The Changing Shape
of Protestantism
in the South

The Changing Shape
of Protestantism
in the South

Edited by Marion D. Aldridge and Kevin Lewis

Mercer University Press
Macon, Georgia

ISBN 0-86554-518-9————————————————————————————

The Changing Shape of Protestantism in the South

Edited by Marion D. Aldridge and Kevin Lewis

Copyright 1996
Mercer University Press
6316 Peake Road
Macon, Georgia 31210-3960
(912) 752-2880

Library of Congress Cataloging-in-Publication Data

The changing shape of Protestantism in the South / edited by Marion D.
Aldridge and Kevin Lewis.
    viii + 88 pp.   6 x 9" (15 x 23 cm.)
    Lectures from a conference held in Mar. 1995 in Columbia, S. C.
    Includes bibliographical references.
    ISBN 0-86554-518-9 (alk. paper)
    1. Protestant churches—Southern States—Congresses. 2. Southern
States—Religious life and customs—Congresses. I. Aldridge, Marion D.,
1947–   . II. Lewis, Kevin, 1943–   .
BR535.C43 1996
280'.4'097509049—dc20   96–30445
                                                                                            CIP

Contents

Preface

This volume is meant for both church and academy. Our respective comments at the beginning and end, like bookends, signal a collaborative effort to bring the contents to a mixed audience. We believe these chapters will attract readers in the pastor's study and in the library cubicle alike, in the pew and in the classroom, in seminaries and in departments of religious studies.

The voices in this collection do not sound alike. This is both result and symptom of change within Southern Protestantism. No longer is "church" predictable. Its leadership now includes women, African-Americans, market-driven evangelists, charismatics, and a host of others who infuse new meaning into old forms—as when intentionally comfortable worship, casually accepted, is now labeled "user friendly." Indeed, old traditions are being recovered (such as house churches), and entirely new experiences are emerging as Protestantism blends, for good or ill, with native American, Muslim, New Age, and Goddess traditions.

In the future, Protestantism in the region may come to be understood more widely as the plural noun, "Protestantisms." Today more than ever, no one voice, no one perspective can be relied upon to tell us all we would like to know about the subject. Many more voices than these of our contributors are needed and welcome.

The regional dimension addressed in this volume will become equally difficult to define in the years ahead. The South is becoming less and less distinct as a culture. This, too, is a result and a sign of the changes that are taking place. Our contributors raise questions about the impact of social and cultural change on the Protestant churches of the South and suggest how to frame answers. They speak not only to the churches as institutions but to the people of the region who are living through these changes as they live out their ever-evolving engagement with Christian faith.

Marion D. Aldridge
Kevin Lewis

Introduction ─────────────────

Marion D. Aldridge

From generation to generation, habits, customs, clothing, language, art, music, and governments all change. Even virtue and vice seem to take on different forms in different times and places. In nearly five decades of my life, all lived in the South, all within the confines of the Methodist and Baptist traditions, I have watched tradition after tradition, some of which we thought were immutable, fall by the wayside. In my adolescence, women would have stayed home from church rather than wear pants to Sunday worship. Yet, recently, the "traditional" Southern Baptist congregation of which I am pastor sponsored a "Caribbean Sunday," and women in pants did not create even a mild stir. The minister of music, however, decked out in Bermuda shorts to lead the morning hymns, created quite a body of commentary!

Whatever our weaknesses and strengths as Southern Protestants, we will reflect the uniqueness of our culture. Cultures, however, vary significantly in different locations and even in different decades in the same location. Changes in the culture of the South inevitably affect the shape of Protestantism in the South. Thus, the task of a conference held in March 1995 in Columbia, South Carolina, was to wrestle with the query, "In what way is Southern Protestantism changing as we approach the twenty-first century?" What are Southern Protestants thinking and doing these days, and how are these things different (if, indeed, they are distinct) from what they and other Christians have believed and done in years past?

The Center on Religion in the South, a kind of religious "think tank" located in Columbia, South Carolina, on the campus of the Lutheran Theological Southern Seminary, decided to ask those questions of several of the world's leading scholars whose focus is the discipline of Southern religion and culture. They were asked to give their perspectives on the question of how Protestant life has changed in the Southern portion of the United States in the last few decades. The Center, headed by Paul Jersild, organized a conference, open to both scholars and front-line ecclesiastical practitioners, for the purpose of such a discussion. The Center, with the substantial financial assistance of the Louisville Institute for the Study of Protestantism and American Culture, attracted a national audience and provided a wonderful forum for lively, and often humorous, discussion concerning religious life in the South.

Wade Clark Roof, the J. F. Rowny Professor of Religion and Society at the University of California, Santa Barbara, was the keynote speaker. He is internationally recognized for his study of Baby Boomers and Religion, and is a native of Columbia, South Carolina, where the conference was held. In his lecture, "Southern Protestantism: New Challenges, New Possibilities," Roof argues that a new pluralism and a frank individualism are the predominant sources of change within the region's religion. He also discusses the widening gap between the churched and the unchurched, marketing strategies of the church, and new organizational forms which the church is appropriating.

Other speakers, and contributors to this volume, include William H. Willimon, dean of the chapel and professor of Christian ministry at Duke University; Bill Leonard, professor of Religion and chair of the department of Religion and Philosophy at Samford University; Larry Mamiya, professor of Religion and African Studies at Vassar College; and Nancy Hardesty, visiting associate professor of Philosophy and Religion at Clemson University. Each of these scholars is a respected interpreter of life within some particular segment of the church, especially some aspect of the Protestant church in the South.

Willimon, in a lecture titled "On Being a Christian and a Southerner at the Same Time," develops the thesis, through narrative, that a Southerner's self-identity is formed in large part by the tragedy of its regional history, especially with regard to slavery. Leonard, a Southern Baptist, uses his own denomination as a case study for the changes within Southern Protestantism. His lecture, "One Denomination, Many Centers," contends that Baptists in the South are returning to an old method of relating with one another, local churches cooperating (or networking) independently with societies (*e.g.*, "mission delivery" organizations) as they deem appropriate, a grass-roots approach to missions and education, and moving from the more rigid and more bureaucratic "convention" model in which decisions are made at the regional or national level and passed "down" for congregational consumption. Mamiya outlines the places where black religion in the South is experiencing change. Titling his lecture "Black Churches and the Emerging Challenges in the Twenty-first Century," Mamiya notes that growing poverty, the neo-Pentecostal movement, nondenominational megachurches, and Islam all are having an impact on the future of black Southern Protestantism. Hardesty's title, "From Religion to Spirituality: Southern Women in and out of the Church," is a clue to her lecture's content. She believes that the underrepresentation of women in the leadership of the church has impoverished the church, and that women will insist, in the future, that they either have a place within the hierarchy of the church or that they will create organizations (for example, house churches) where they can relate to one another and to God in ways that are meaningful to them.

Additionally, a diverse panel of area pastors was enlisted to conclude the conference by having them reflect on the changes taking place within the churches from their perspectives as active clergy within the local church. Each had valuable insights unique to his or her peculiar perspective. Joe Darby, a pastor to a rural congregation in the African Methodist Episcopal tradition said, "I see a resurgence and a returning to church by black people who have need for a nurturer and advocate. With conservative politics in the ascendancy, my people come to church because they need to talk to Jesus more." Marshall Edwards, a Southern Baptist pastor of a suburban megachurch, affiliated with both the Southern Baptist Convention and the Cooperative Baptist Fellowship, said, "We need to deal with pain in the church, whether it is feminist or racial. We'll see a huge dying away of what we have been in the past." Denise Childress, a United Methodist pastor in a small, South Carolina community, said, "Preaching the gospel is to invite change. An example of that would be gender issues." Sam Candler, dean of Episcopal Trinity Cathedral in downtown Columbia, said, "Change will happen as long as people are coming to church. Our doors need to be wide open. We all carry baggage. We need the 'other' to show us Christ. We need to abandon some of our established styles of leadership and methodology."

In reviewing the data from the conference, I realized that the analysis of the possible relationships between the church and secular culture described by H. Richard Niebuhr in his classic volume, *Christ and Culture*, though mentioned, was never developed. A familiarity with his formulas is helpful to any serious student of the Christian church. Niebuhr's general outline is worth reviewing here as a backdrop to the discussion.

While Niebuhr presents other options, the "Big Three" methods in which Christ and Culture have related historically are these: (1) Christ is identified with Culture: God is on our country's or our region's side! When we decide on a philosophy or an action, God surely approves. (2) Christ and culture are in conflict: God is never on the side of any secular society. The church, to be true to its calling, must be set apart from the prevailing practices of the general public. (3) Christ calls Christians to transform culture: God loves the created world, but it is not perfect, and God's people must be about the task of changing the world to reflect more closely the kingdom of God.

Roof, though not arguing that the South completely identifies its church with its region, does consider Southern religion to be a "Christ-and-culture blend" making it "virtually impossible to understand one without the other." He observes that, in times past, unchurched Southerners looked pretty much like those who regularly attended church. One of the major changes in Southern Protestantism, according to Roof, is that "the church no longer enjoys the cultural props."

The culture has moved away from the church rather than vice versa. (This is a safe assumption since, as Leonard argued in the discussion following his lecture, Baptists, the largest denomination in the South, "would rather die than change." Mamiya, commenting on the black experience agrees that there is an increasing distance between the church and the prevailing culture of its constituents. He contends that the black poor are alienated from all institutions, including the church. Hardesty also concurs with the concept of an increasing estrangement between the Southern Protestant church and its culture: "Working outside the home and still shouldering most of the burden for the work within the home, many women are just too tired to bother with the church any more.") This change in status means there is need for serious reflection about what happens next to the Christian church in the Southern region of the United States.

The various analyses of how the practice of the Protestant faith in the South has changed and will change reflected the theme, consistently heard throughout the conference, that Southern religion is not as uniquely and distinctively Southern as it once was (The five-second television sound byte has affected us all.), though the region still has its own flavor. Will Willimon reminded us: "You know you were conceived in sin if you are a Southerner. We got caught red-handed!"

This generation, nationally and regionally, seems to have, as Sam Candler pointed out in the panel discussion at the close of the conference, a fascination with the pelvic issues, defined as the ordination of women, abortion, and homosexuality. Yet, in the formal presentations, these topics were largely ignored, except as the lecturers theorized that, increasingly, the concerns of Southern Protestantism are more and more similar to the issues facing the rest of religious America.

A related theme that emerged with some frequency throughout the conference was the proposition that this generation of Southerners is less connected to their history, their family, and their church and is more autonomous than past generations. Cultural pressure to act in a certain way, moral or otherwise, is, to some degree, less than in the past, and the "do your own thing" mentality that was talked about in the 1970s is actually in place and functioning in the 1990s. Consequently, people come to church to get their own needs met, not to be challenged morally. Or, they attend church to find a place for fellowship with like-minded believers. If Church A doesn't meet their needs, then they will try Church B. If Church B doesn't meet their needs, they will try the garden club or the service club or a parachurch organization or a twelve-step group or none of the above. During the question-and-answer session after his address, Bill Leonard referred to the megachurch pastor who said, "We'll baptize by immersion if that's what they want. We will sprinkle if that's what they want. We'll baptize babies if that's what they want. We don't want baptism to keep someone from following Jesus." In a similar vein, Will Willimon remarked, "We woke up one day and couldn't tell the difference between church and Rotary. Rotary at least meets on a convenient day of the week and serves lunch."

The tension between responding appropriately to culture for evangelistic purposes and resisting the mimicking of cultural mores was a constant theme of the conference. It is one with which I, as a pastor, must wrestle every day.

Churches that are trying to get the pulse of the world, and then attempting to adjust their activities to the heartbeat of hard hearts, had better be careful. Talking with a pastor friend recently, I was confessing my envy of the phenomenal growth of some other churches. His word of wisdom for me was that the pastors of megachurches, not I, ought to be the ones who are sleepless at night. Anyone who is building a church on the prevailing wind of public opinion had better be nervous, because public opinion shifts like the breeze.

Our assignment, as churches, is not to create a Wal-Mart Community Church, where the aisles are wide, the merchandising is slick, the message is comfortable, and the price of salvation is a little cheaper.

Living in this world is like fitting a square peg into a round hole. It is like butting our collective heads up against a wall. The list of images and metaphors to describe the pain that we cause to God, to ourselves, and to one another when we abandon God's ways for the world's ways is almost endless. Shakespeare knew it, so he wrote tragedies that said things like, "The time is out of joint." The prophets and the apostles knew it, and, inspired by God, they spoke bluntly of human sinfulness. Here are the words of the apostle Paul in 1 Corinthians 1:27: "God chose what is foolish in the world to shame the wise; God chose what is weak in the world to shame the strong." God's ways and human ways are, often, directly at odds with each other. Even secular writers like Michael Crichton, author of *Jurassic Park*, understand this dilemma. In the sequel to *Jurassic Park*, a book called *The Lost World*, Crichton has a character complain about the difficulty of protecting human beings from their own mistakes: "How can you design for people, if you don't know history and psychology? You can't. Because your mathematical formulas may be perfect, but the people will screw it up."

A study of the Old Testament reveals more of the same. God's prophet Amos had to speak against the king's prophet, Amaziah. Amaziah reflected the values and opinions of the culture whereas Amos spoke for the morality and spirituality required by God. The great temptation has always been to make God in our image! Roof took on the mantle of the prophet when he said that Southern Protestants "will need to reflect upon their own heritages and offer a viable and authentic Gospel, and not lose that viability and authenticity in worries about how best to package the product to make it sell in a consumption-oriented society."

Furthermore, as a pastor of a local church, I wonder, as I attempt to work in a heterogeneous congregation made up of Republicans and Democrats, liberals and conservatives, how I should responsibly interpret cultural issues, on which there are diverse opinions, so that the institution that pays my salary is not destroyed? These were not and are not merely theoretical questions to me and to the dozens of other ecclesiastical practitioners in the conference's audience. Maybe the task is impossible.

Maybe it has always been impossible, and that is why institutional religion has, for centuries, had a love-hate relationship with its prophets and its leadership. I watched a movie recently (*Reality Bytes*) in which one of the characters, a young man, said, "I am not under any orders to make the world a better place." That, according to the theology of original sin, has always has been the philosophy of the bulk of humanity.

Such self-centeredness is also the challenge of the church in the years immediately ahead. The prospects seem ominous. How do we coalesce hundreds (or even dozens) of people around the common theme of sacrifice when we have been taught by the world to "Look out for number one"? This tutorial in self-care is a lesson people, including Southerners, including Southern Protestants, have learned well.

Commenting on the harsh, negative stances of some churches, Hardesty asked, "What do people get out of it? If I want to hear just negative things about myself, I can watch commercials on TV. I will not go to a church that abuses me."

One of the most fascinating exchanges of the two-day event transpired when Nancy Hardesty was fielding questions after her lecture regarding the spiritual issues of Southern women. My good friend Joe Darby, an African-American, leaned over and whispered to me that he was somewhat uncomfortable with the way women's rights and black issues were being woven together, an opinion I have heard from other African-Americans. The argument for the disconnection would be that the issues faced by blacks in our society should not be confused with or diluted by other moral concerns or agendas, no matter how important the issue or how convenient the connection. The concerns of African-Americans are unique! A few moments later, someone asked Hardesty, "Why don't women get more involved in the flag issue?" [The "flag issue" in South Carolina, in a nutshell, is this: One of the flags of the Confederacy, placed over our state house during the Civil Rights struggles of the 1960s, still flies there along with the flags of the United States and the state of South Carolina. Its presence, obviously, is an affront to our state's black citizens.] Hardesty's answer was a perfect parallel to Darby's whispered comment to me. She said, "There are more important issues to women." Here were two good friends, respected leaders in the Christian community of our state, each with an understandable but narrow focus on his or her own issue. Their calls for justice in their respective areas of interest are quite valid. Yet, these two Southern

Protestants are products of the cultures that molded them, as I am, and that means they have the capacity to be more interested in the restricted concerns of their subgroup than with the more general interests of the larger cultural unit.

Like much else we heard during the course of the conference, these are single issue interests. If our best and brightest are immersed eyeball-deep in their own particular predicaments, how can we reasonably expect cliché-driven laypeople, dominated as their thinking is by the five-second sound byte, to develop a broader understanding of the issues we face.

I recently heard someone warn a group of Christians not to "back into the future by looking forward to the past." If you are going to adopt a cliché, that is a good one! Christians, on the heaven side of Easter, should feel confidence about the future. Let those who do not know Jesus be timid, fearful, and anxious. People who cannot move into the future with confidence are those who think that life has already peaked, that the best God has to offer is in the past.

That goes contrary to the Easter message that Jesus has risen and is going before us. We are not alone. The life and ministry of Jesus are not limited to what has already transpired. As Christians, we must not be merely nostalgic, clinging to tradition, hankering for the good ol' days. In Jesus, Christians have hope for the future. A common theme of the world outside the church is mere survival, people hoping they can hang on: "If only things will not change too much!" Within the church, Christian people are called to embrace the new, to repent (resulting in change in their own lives) *and* to be agents of transformation within society.

Many churches have died, hanging onto the past. I heard Walter Bruggemann, Old Testament scholar and modern day prophet, say that the single great fact for ministry as we approach the end of the millennium is the collapse of the white, male leadership that has governed our culture for centuries. When we have church members who say, "Preacher, my wife has been transferred to the West Coast," then we know things have changed from the way they used to be. Can God go with us, as a church and as individuals, to those places we have never been before? Of course God can. Is it confusing? Of course it is.

Hanging onto the past has a long and distinguished history! It is in the Bible from cover to cover. Isaiah, the prophet, in Isaiah 43:18, told God's people, "Stop dwelling on past events and brooding over days gone by." In the next verse, God, speaking through Isaiah, said, "I am about to do something new!"

Do you remember the story of Lot's wife? God had given Lot's family the opportunity to start fresh, to begin again. They had fled the sinful city of Sodom (Genesis 19:26), but Lot's wife, resisting the future, nostalgic for the things of her past, looked back, and the Bible tells us she turned into a pillar of salt.

Do you remember the Hebrew children in the wilderness, complaining to Moses about the way things used to be? "If only we had meat to eat! We remember the fish we used to eat in Egypt for nothing, the cucumbers, the melons, the leeks, the onions, and the garlic. . . . How happy we were in Egypt" (Numbers 11:5,6,18). They conveniently forgot that they had been slaves in Egypt.

Jesus picks up the same theme in Luke 9:62: "No one who puts a hand to the plough and then looks back is fit for the kingdom of God."

Change is not the enemy any more than culture is the enemy. Roof sounds a note of hope for the Southern Protestant church as it becomes less identified with its culture than it has been in the past: "My reading of American religious history suggests that at every stage along the way, when religious groups have become less established, and more reliant upon their voluntary efforts, they have become more, not less, influential. One of the fundamental axioms of contemporary sociology of religion is that religious monopolies of the sort that once existed in the South inevitably will become lazy monopolies; and that by contrast, religious pluralism and competition are signs of religious vitality." He concludes, "Loss of establishment-status may well be invigorating."

Southern Protestantism: New Challenges, New Possibilities

Wade Clark Roof

Religion in the South—not unlike the Southern region as a whole—is usually looked upon from the vantage point of its distinctiveness, with emphasis more on its continuity with the past than its recent change. Southerners themselves, in fact, have preferred to talk about continuity rather than change. As W. J. Cash so eloquently described many years ago in his little classic, *The Mind of the South*, pressures have been strong upon Southern whites to uphold a vision and myth of cultural tradition, if for no other reason than as a means for confronting the many irruptions that threatened it.

Of course, there has been much continuity. Books about the pervasiveness of Southern life and culture, including its religious life, have been legion—one thinks of such titles as "the lasting South" and "the enduring South." Even today, the region has more churches per thousand population than anywhere else in the country, maybe even in the world. It especially has Protestant churches—Baptist and Methodist, notably Baptist—enough to prompt America's well-known religious commentator, Martin E. Marty, once to remark that there were more Baptists in the South than people. His comment was not just about the region's religious demography, but about its popular religious culture. The South remains distinctively religious, as measured by its evangelical piety, its emotional fervor, its highly personal moral orientation. While such qualities are found elsewhere, of course, seldom are they found to the same degree or in quite the same configuration as in Dixie.

Yet for all its distinctiveness and continuity, change in the contemporary South is the far more important story. These two are encountered in everyday life, of course, not as distinct opposites, but more as a blend of experiences and realities. The South, while still definably distinct as a cultural region, looks more like the rest of the country with each passing year. Historian C. Van Woodward speaks of "the bulldozer revolution," an economic revolution that came late to the South, but when it did, it rapidly began to transform the region's landscape. Interstate highways, shopping malls, and fast-food chains invaded the South as anywhere else. The locus of change is no longer just the nation, of course. Ours is a global world where the investment dollars reach far and wide. For example, I was struck to find in reading *The Chronicle of Higher Education* recently, an advertizement looking for an administrator at the University of South Carolina at Spartanburg, which noted that the Piedmont area of South Carolina is now the area of the nation with the greatest concentration of European investment!

Given all of this social, economic, and cultural change, what is happening to religion? More specifically, what is happening to Southern Protestantism? My reflections on these questions are in three parts: first, and very briefly, I shall offer a cultural perspective upon Southern religion; then I shall describe some of the major religious changes in the country since the 1960s, with attention to how these are playing out in the South; and finally, I shall offer a concluding commentary about how the South may yet provide a sustainable mode of life in the new, postmodern world now breaking in upon us as we approach the turn of a century.

I

Let us look first, then, at the cultural perspective. Here I draw heavily off Samuel S. Hill, Jr.'s pioneering studies of Southern religion some thirty years ago.[1] Hill argued that as a starting point, we ought to recognize that the South has two cultures—one having to do with "being religious" and the other with "being southern." Further, he argued that one must grasp the bonds linking these two if we are to grasp the very core of Southern religion. His was a Durkheimian approach that emphasized the very close

---

[1]See Samuel S. Hill, Jr., *Southern Churches in Crisis* (New York: Hold, Rinehart and Winston, 1966) and Samuel S. Hill, Jr. with Edgar T. Thompson, Anne Firor Scott, Charles Hudson, and Edwin S. Gaustad, *Religion and the Solid South* (Nashville: Abingdon, 1972).

relations between religion and regionality. In H. Richard Niebuhr's well-known categories, he was emphasizing a Christ-and-culture blend in the South that made it virtually impossible to understand one without the other.

His argument held especially for what he called "popular Southern Protestantism," most notably the white Baptist and Methodist memberships, which at the time he wrote amounted to upwards of eighty percent of the population in some Southern states. Together, these two large bodies constituted a religious empire where regional faith and culture were most harmonious, and where the tenets of Christianity were filtered through the history and experiences of the people. Other Protestant bodies —especially the adventists, Pentecostals, and Holiness sectarians—were more on the periphery, as were Catholics and Jews. The religion of Baptists and Methodists set the agenda, in part because of their great size and also because of their affinity with the culture. "Popular southern religion" persists as core-cultural: recently I received a church bulletin from a United Methodist church in Georgia, which carries a list of comments on Christian virtues offered by Billy Graham, Jesus Christ, Pearl Bailey, Robert E. Lee, and Naomi Judd, in that order! Where else in Christendom would this happen?

Southerners have had their own religious story—one born out of the region's peculiar history and experiences, a story principally of conversion and salvation of individuals. In the words of journalist Marshall Frady, himself a southerner, popular religion in the South has been "a romance about the Cross—a dire melodrama of thorns and betrayal and midnight anguish, with nothing in the life of Jesus mattering quite so much as his suffering and his death."[2] Novelist Flannery O'Connor implied as much when she spoke of the South as "Christ-haunted." Everything else found in Christendom—liturgy, meditation, conception of the church, a social ethic—was made secondary to this drama of the lost individual standing before the Almighty desperately in need of conversion. So whether in terms of ecclesiology, Christology, or cultural ethos, Dixie's version of religion has been, and to some extent still is, rather peculiar. As John Shelton Reed writes, paraphrasing Irving Babbitt's observation about the Spanish, there seems to be something

---

[2]Marshall Frady, *Southerners: A Journalist's Odyssey* (New York: Meridian Books, 1980) xv-xvi.

Southern about Southerners that causes them to behave in a Southern manner.[3]

But even at the time Hill was writing, questions arose about whether this popular religious culture would survive. He wondered about what might happen to this blend of religiousness and southerness in a time of rapid social change. Surveying the scene in the mid-1960s—amidst the racial crisis, protests of the Vietnam War, and the early noises of a gender revolution in the making—Hill pondered the possibility that the old cultural bonds in the South might actually break down. Hence the title of his book published in 1966, *Southern Churches in Crisis*. In a subsequent volume entitled *Religion and the Solid South,* Hill wrote: "As Southerness becomes less important, uncritical subscription and loyalty to church religion is apt to follow a parallel course. This constitutes the crisis of the Southern churches."[4] There was, he wrote, "a radically different age and climate" lying ahead, though he was unclear at the time how the churches would respond to the challenges on the horizon.

So it is entirely appropriate to take a second look at the religious situation today. Now three decades later, many of the challenges Hill foresaw have materialized. The South has passed through the racial crisis, though it has hardly solved the problem of racism. Members of the noisy 1960s student generation are now in midlife, and many of the changes in values and lifestyles that they spearheaded as youth are widely spread throughout American society in the 1990s. These are values that many now take for granted, both among those who are older and for Generation Xers now entering adulthood. I speak of such values as greater racial and gender equality, concern for self-fulfillment, quality of life, tolerance of alternative lifestyles, concern for the environment, a more open, relativistic view toward matters of faith and commitment. These are all values of a post-World War II baby boom generation, a generation that has greatly altered all of America's social institutions—including religious institutions. I shall argue that these generational changes in values are at the forefront of religious change in the South and elsewhere today.

---

[3]John Shelton Reed, *One South: An Ethnic Approach to Regional Culture* (Baton Rouge LA: Louisiana State University Press, 1982) 131.

[4]Hill, "The South's Two Cultures," in *Religion and the Solid South,* 54.

II

So then, how is Southern Protestantism faring today? The question prompts answers at two levels. One answer is that it is doing pretty well. Compared with other parts of the country, Protestantism fares better in this region and has fewer challenges from other faiths or from the encroachments of secular ideology. A second answer is more guarded. When it is said that Southern Protestantism is faring well, that simply means that by comparison with other parts of the country, the historic Southern Protestant churches continue to have a fairly strong hold upon the culture. The "restructuring" of American Protestantism, to use Robert Wuthnow's term,[5] has been nothing short of massive—yet far less massive in the South. The latest data on religion's market shares suggest the following: (1) theologically liberal and moderate mainline denominations have both lost members in all the regions of the U.S., but the losses have been less in the South than anywhere else; (2) theologically conservative denominations have grown in most regions—about the same in the South elsewhere; (3) the fastest-growing religious groups in all the regions are the Pentecostal and Holiness bodies.[6] The growth of the Pentecostal and Holiness groups is truly phenomenal, not just on this continent but in Central and South America as well, as described in Harvey Cox's *Fire From Heaven.*[7] Along with Pentecostal and Holiness groups, nondenominational and community churches are growing at a rapid pace—of all the "isms" that flourish today, clearly denominationalism is not one of them.

Moreover, the religious economy has greatly changed in the South since Hill's time. Perhaps the most visible change in the religious economy is the upward social movement of what was once called the Southern sectarians—the Pentecostals, Adventists, and Holiness groups. Vance Packard, in his 1959 best-seller, *The Status Seekers,* spoke of "The

---

[5]Robert Wuthnow, *The Restructuring of American Religion* (Princeton: Princeton University Press, 1988).

[6]These trends are summarized in David A. Roozen, "Denominations Grow as Individuals Join Congregations," 15-35 in David A. Roozen and C. Kirk Hadaway, *Church and Denominational Growth* (Nashville: Abingdon, 1993).

[7]Harvey Cox, *Fire from Heaven* (Reading MA: Addison-Wesley, 1995).

Long Road from Pentecostal to Episcopal."[8] But today, that road has shortened considerably. Better education, professionalization, and upward social mobility have led many of them to a higher religious ground. Likewise, the technological and computer revolutions have created new religious sounds resonating to the tastes of many persons wanting a more experiential style of faith. The result is a new brand of popular Protestantism laying claim on the mainstream culture, leaving behind old sectarian traits, and appearing more prosperous. Given these broad cultural and religious changes, combined with the powerful evangelical movement across the country, Baptists and Methodists no longer constitute the religious empire they once did in the South. Put simply, the old Southern mainline no longer enjoys the privileged status it once held.

Other types of indicators are worth noting, too, in pointing us toward a greater sweep of religious changes now underway:

(1) One is the new religious pluralism. By new pluralism, I refer to the expanding diversity of faiths across the country. The history of Christianity in America, of course, can be interpreted as an expanding pluralism: first there were Protestants, in many stripes; then added were Catholics and Jews, also in many stripes. By the 1950s, we were as Will Herberg said a "Protestant-Catholic-Jewish" country.[9] But by the 1990s, Herberg's formulation had become too narrow—left out were the Muslims, one of the fastest growing religious groups in the country, and hundreds of other smaller groups.

Actually, the last couple of decades have been a time of exploding new religions in the United States, including many new Christian denominations. I refer mainly to the growth of new ethnic denominations such as the Korean Presbyterians, Latino Pentecostals, Cape Verdian Catholics, and Cambodian Methodists. These groups have mushroomed since the mid-1960s when the liberalization of immigration laws opened the gates to a massive population movement that is reshaping American culture. It may well be in the long reach of this country's history that the Immigration Reform Act of 1965 will be remembered as the twin and equal of the Civil Rights Act of 1964—ushering in a more global mix of peoples and cultures. Especially in our cities, we now see this emerging

---

[8]Vance Packard, *The Status Seekers* (New York: David McKay Company, 1959).
[9]Will Herberg, *Protestant-Catholic-Jew* (Garden City NY: Doubleday Anchor, 1960).

mix of faiths and emergent forms of racial and ethnic Christianity, unlike the older Euro-American expressions of religious communities.[10]

How does all of this play out in the South? For sure, there is less evidence of a global transformation here than in some other places. But the rapid growth of Latino and Asian groups in the larger Southern cities should not be underestimated. Check out the names in phone books in places such as Atlanta, Charlotte, and Birmingham—not to mention Miami, of course. You might be surprised. Atlanta, so I am told, has a rapidly growing Hindu population. In many Southern cities, Vietnamese populations are on the rise. Also, there are movements like Wicca and Goddess worship—groups that push the boundaries of pluralism out even further. The evidence on these new religions suggests that they are far more widespread than we generally recognize; unless you hang out at New Age bookstores, you aren't likely to realize just how widespread many of these new spiritual teachings are. In our survey on baby boomers, for example, roughly one-fourth of the young Americans we interviewed said they believed in reincarnation—the figures are not all that lower in the South. In California and Massachusetts it was three out of ten, in North Carolina two out of ten.[11]

It strikes me that Southerners are poised on the threshold of a new era for exploring "religious others." White Southerners are getting to know black Southerners in a more genuine way and to appreciate alternative styles of faith and spirituality. Now the challenge is to expand the horizons even further.

(2) Another type of pluralism is the growing split between the churched and the unchurched. Somewhat more than forty percent of Americans as a whole fit into the category of the unchurched—those having little, if any, involvement within organized religion. Figures in the South are less for the unchurched, but again, the differences are not as great as might be expected. The Gallup Unchurched Study some years ago revealed that the South was just a couple of percentage points lower than the Midwest, which was a few points lower than the East, which

---

[10]See Wade Clark Roof, "Toward Year 2000: Reconstructions of Religious Space," *Annals of the American Academy of Political and Social Science* 527 (May 1993): 155-70.

[11]Wade Clark Roof, *A Generation of Seekers* (San Francisco: Harper SanFrancisco, 1993).

was lower than the West.[12] A general profile of the unchurched appears to be emerging across the country: the unchurched are younger, better educated, urban, geographically mobile, more computer literate, more likely to be members of the so-called "knowledge class," those who create, disseminate, and interpret information in our increasingly information-oriented society.

This development in the class structure is of great significance. It signals a shift in the relation of the unchurched to the culture—whereas the unchurched were once more a marginal group, now they enjoy a more culturally respectable position. The rise of the "knowledge class" also points to a new cleavage in the New South—that of the churched versus the unchurched. Those who were unchurched have long been in the South, of course, but in the past they looked pretty much like the churched in their values and lifestyles, except that they didn't go to church. Now the profile is changing. Especially in the urban South, a cleavage between the churched and unchurched cultures is becoming more visible. Research suggests that differences between the two in friendship patterns, in moral and religious values, and in lifestyles are on the increase.[13] A key indicator are attitudes toward the churches. Once the Southern unchurched were respectful of religion even if not involved, but that is less true today. Southerners outside the church are as critical today, if not more so, of organized religion as non-Southerners. To put it differently, the church no longer enjoys the cultural props in the way it once did; there was a time when the culture was friendly and supportive, but now it is more indifferent, if not openly hostile.

(3) Another national trend is what William McKinney and I have called the "new voluntarism."[14] The new voluntarism is the trend toward turning inward, toward individual choice, toward pick-and-choose Christianity. It has to do with the greater authority claimed by the individual believer to decide for herself what to believe and how to practice

---

[12]See my article, "Religious Change in the American South: The Case of the Unchurched," 192-210 in Samuel S. Hill, ed., *Varieties of Southern Religious Experience* (Baton Rouge LA: Louisiana State University Press, 1988).

[13]For a review of research findings, see my article "Religious Change in the American South: The Case of the Unchurched."

[14]Wade Clark Roof and William J. McKinney, *American Mainline Religion: Its Changing Shape and Future* (New Brunswick NJ: Rutgers University Press, 1987).

faith—what Canadian sociologist Reginald Bibby refers to as "religion à la carte."[15] It is perhaps the most insidious, most challenging of all the contemporary trends, in eroding religious commitment.

In American religious life, this trend expresses itself in a variety of ways. People decide for themselves whether church-going is important for them; the churches themselves have by and large lost the power to enforce the norms. The fact is that eight out of ten Americans generally in Gallup surveys say "One can be a good Christian without going to church." Protestant or Catholic, mainliner or evangelical, Southerner or non-Southerner, all are about the same. Views on church-going have become, as Peter Berger says, "privatized."[16]

We observe high levels of religious switching from one denomination to another—movement that leads to regrouping, more on the grounds of personal choice and conviction rather than sticking with family heritage. There is both choice of new religions and choice of interpretation within religion. Andrew Greeley speaks of "selective Catholicism;" among Protestants there are new blends of faith and culture—such as vegetarian Unitarians, Quakerpalians, or Lake Wobegon Lutherans. The drift is in the direction of combining lifestyle or experiential meaning with denominational labels.

Overall, loyalty to religious denominations is on the decline, and especially so among the more established, oldline denominations. Declining loyalty is expressed often in subtle ways: in the weakened attachments to congregations, in less clarity of denominational identities. For baby boomers and Generation Xers in particular, ties to existing institutions have greatly eroded.

Robert Bellah and others have commented at length on the dangers of a growing religious individualism leading to the erosion of religious tradition and institutional belonging. Almost everyone has heard of "Sheilaism" from Bellah *et al.'s* work. A person interviewed in that study, Sheila Larson, used the term "Sheilaism" to describe her own

---

[15]Reginald W. Bibby, *Fragmented Gods: The Poverty and Potential of Religion in Canada* (Toronto: Irwin Publishing, 1987).

[16]The notion of "privatization" is developed in Peter L. Berger, *The Sacred Canopy* (Garden City NY: Doubleday, 1967).

deeply individualistic and highly internalized mode of religion.[17] Sheila has many spiritual kin of one type or another. To the extent that Sheilaism refers simply to inner conscience, totally cut off from belief in an external reality, that is indeed a serious challenge to the historic Christian faiths.

Much of this discussion, however, is misfocused. If by Sheilaism we mean a respect for the inner voice, then of course from the time of Emerson and the Transcendentalists to the present there has been a strand of religious thought in this country that has emphasized the divine truth that comes from within. This strand of religion is much more common in New England and on the West Coast than in the South—and thus for this reason, the arrival of New Age thinking (and its older version, called New Thought) here in the South marks even more of a departure from tradition than is the case elsewhere. High levels of individualism will no doubt contribute to the undermining of Southern religious culture as we have known it in the past, especially its reliance upon custom and family heritage as carriers of tradition. Southerners, as people elsewhere, will want to believe for themselves.

But as is often the case, this is both bad news and good news. If the force of custom and tradition is on the decline, it is also true that a new-style of individualism in Southern life may yield very positive religious benefits: Greater choice in matters of faith should lead to greater clarity of what one actually believes; it should lead as well to greater personal responsibility for faith and commitment. Just because there is more free choice doesn't mean that people will necessarily decide against religion, they might actually decide for religion. Believing for oneself, rather than believing simply out of custom or family heritage, can be a creative process, and something religious institutions might actually encourage. Some church memberships will decline in a more open religious market, but others will grow. Individuals will enjoy greater freedom to switch from one congregation to another, or from one denomination to another, but that will help to create a religious system more in keeping with people's own preferences and commitments. In the long run, that should lead to a more intentional, self-consciously aware church that relies more

---

[17]Robert N. Bellah, Richard Madsen, William M. Sullivan, Ann Swidler, and Steven M. Tipton, *Habits of the Heart: Individualism and Commitment in American Life* (Berkeley: University of California Press, 1985).

on the resources of faith, and less on cultural mores and custom, to keep it alive and present in the world.

A second thing can be said about the exercise of greater religious choice: With choice and more openness comes a greater awareness about the place of the spiritual. For some, this heightened awareness of the spiritual leads to personal journeys, self-initiated and self-charted pilgrimages that perhaps will take them out of ordinary religious routines. I think of a young, career woman in North Carolina who told us she found it necessary to take a "leave of absence" from her church for a while in order to form a support group with other women to explore their female spirituality. Groups such as that are popping up all over the country as women break out of old roles and routines and define for themselves who they are in ways allowing them to explore their inner lives. Mainline Protestantism in the South should not fear the gender revolution, but instead find ways to encourage the rich female spirituality now rising to the surface after so long a period of male domination.

For others exercising this new religious choice, there is awareness of a spiritual void and acknowledgment of a deep hunger for something to fill that void. Time and time again in our interviews with baby boomers across the country, we were struck with the depths of people's spiritual quests. Partly this is a matter of age. Demographically, large numbers in this generation are in their forties—a time of midlife transitions when people ask questions about who they are and what they are doing. An aging cohort is asking questions about work in a rapidly changing economy, about family life in a time when the family as an institution is facing severe problems, and about the meaning of life itself when many of the once taken-for-granted certainties seem to have dissolved. Even the certainties once associated with religious institutions have dissolved for some—leaving them with only their own inner spaces. Signs of quest and ferment are evident in many places: check the best-seller book lists of the major newspapers across the country, or the growth of spiritual retreat centers, or simply visit any good bookstore. Notice how much bookshelf space is devoted to journey and recovery spirituality, certainly more space than is given to religion as tradition or institution. Today the culture is turned inward, in search of what can be found within people's lives and experiences.

(4) Another trend is the rise of new organizational structures. New organizational forms are emerging as denominational empires are decen-

tralizing. Not just in religion, but in corporations and government, we see signs of a restlessness with bureaucracy and a spirit of "reinventing" our fundamental institutions. In Wuthnow's view, "restructuring" has meant an increased polarization between liberals and conservatives, an argument that hardly needs to be made in an address to United Methodists, Lutherans, Presbyterians, and especially Southern Baptists today. With polarization has come many new special purpose groups devoted to particular causes, on the left and on the right, such as prison ministries, abortion counseling, concerns about ecology, ministry to persons with AIDS, and so forth. In our time of "culture wars," such causes can, and often do, generate commitments that transcend denominations. We might even go so far as to say that the rise of special purpose organizations has helped to level some of the long-standing differences between denominations, for it is now the case that those with similar views and causes often have more in common across denominations than do members within the same denomination, or perhaps even within the same congregation.

But restructuring has other meanings—one is the phenomenal rise of small groups across America. Indeed, the small-group revolution is far greater than I have up to this point implied. I refer to prayer fellowships, Bible study groups, women's groups, twelve-step groups, singles groups, covenant groups, house churches, and a myriad of other types. Wuthnow found in his recent survey that one out of four Americans is involved in some kind of a small group, most of them religious or spiritual in some way.[18] The survey shows that such groups are only slightly less common in the South than elsewhere. What appears to be happening is a groundswell of spiritual interest in a culture in which spirituality has become a highly private matter, and where many people are turning to small, intentional groups for sharing their life journeys. At a time when the authority of established religious institutions has eroded, when families are not providing the support they once did, when people are feeling a loss of community and widespread uprootedness about their lives, small groups fulfill important roles. According to Wuthnow, many people are joining such groups because they want to deepen their own spirituality. Clearly what is privileged in such groups is one's own personal journeys; creed and doctrine are less important than testimony and biography.

---

[18]Robert Wuthnow, *Sharing the Journey: Support Groups and America's New Quest for Community* (New York: Free Press, 1994).

If Wuthnow is correct, the small-group movement may be having a powerful impact, influencing even our relation to the sacred. Imageries of Deity are undergoing major revision in our time—old notions of patriarchy and judgeship are giving way to softer, more personal conceptions of God. But there may be other, more subtle types of changes in how we think of the divine. In the small-group setting, emphasis is upon journey, upon spiritual growth. The trip for some is better than the destination. Seeking, more so than believing, becomes a major motif. Pragmatic results are more important. As Wuthnow says:

> Spirituality no longer is true or good because it meets absolute standards of truth or goodness, but because it helps me get along. I am the judge of its worth. If it helps me find a vacant parking space, I know my spirituality is on the right track. If it leads me into the wilderness, calling me to face dangers I would rather not deal with at all, then it is a form of spirituality I am unlikely to choose. To be sure, there are significant exceptions to these patterns. Small groups sometimes challenge their members to undertake painful processes of spiritual growth. But the more common pattern seems to be a kind of faith that focuses heavily on feelings and on getting along, rather than encouraging worshipful obedience to or reverence toward a transcendent God.[19]

Another type of restructuring, and one that builds upon small groups, is the church growth movement and the emergence of the megachurch. The church growth movement was made possible by the application of marketing research strategies to the planting of new churches—as workable for churches as for McDonalds. The megachurch is a product of another strategy, making use of a variety of small groups and providing a diversified menu appealing to a culture of choice. Both the church growth movement and the megachurch have flourished in the context of the baby boomer culture, which resonates with choice, small groups, and ironically, anonymity in the large worship setting. The key seems to be finding the right blend of personalism and impersonalism, often combined in a glitzy manner celebrating prosperity.

---

[19]Robert Wuthnow, "Small Groups Force New Notions of Community and the Sacred," *The Christian Century* 110 (8 December 1993): 1239-40.

To many mainliners, much of this seems like religious marketing—which it is. But religious marketing did not begin with the televangelists or the church growth consultants. It's as old as religion in America, for once upon a time the Methodist circuit rider adopted an innovative method of reaching new populations, as was true with the advent of radio ministry and religious publishing ventures. As the South becomes religiously more pluralistic, and thus the religious context more competitive, one would expect that the pressures for religious innovation will likely mount further. If I am correct in this prediction, this may constitute yet another aspect of Hill's crisis of Southern churches. Theologically, the mainline Protestant traditions in the South—that is, the Episcopalians, Presbyterians, Methodists, Baptists, and Lutherans—will need to reflect upon their own heritages and offer a viable and authentic gospel, and not lose that viability and authenticity in worries about how best to package the product to make it sell in a consumption-oriented society.

III

So then, that's my list of major changes reshaping the role of Protestantism in contemporary culture. The new religious economy, greater pluralism, the widening between the churched and the unchurched, new-style voluntarism, new organizational forms, new marketing strategies —all are having an impact on Protestantism in the South. All are challenges for the future.

What about the future possibilities? Envisioning the future is, of course, far more difficult than analyzing the present. Sociologists have a difficult enough time with the present, much less trying to predict what lies ahead. Add to that the distinctive religious history of the South, and the future becomes even less transparent as we try to envision it. But for sure, the national trends that I have described are eroding the old regional religio-cultural complex as Hill suspected would happen. Since his time, the religious climate has become more fluid: people are making religious choices more on their own, bound less by family heritage and tradition. Modernity is often described as a movement "from fate to choice," and that movement is now working itself out in grand fashion in the South. For Southern Protestantism, it means facing a rapidly changing cultural context: new and innovative religious competitors, a growing societal indifference, and the loss of a cultural establishment that it has long relied upon.

But liberation from the culture opens up new possibilities. Some liberation from the "good ol' boys" culture, while at the same time, recognizing and appreciating the new values and experiences of a younger generation of women, of those with alternative life-styles, and of minorities of all kinds, would be a good thing. Religious people in the South might be pleasantly surprised by how invigorated their churches could become by greater inclusiveness. Further, my reading of American religious history suggests that at every stage along the way, when religious groups have become less established and more reliant upon their voluntary efforts, they have become more, not less, influential. One of the fundamental axioms of contemporary sociology of religion is that religious monopolies of the sort that once existed in the South inevitably will become lazy monopolies; by contrast, religious pluralism and competition are signs of religious vitality. If that is the case, then the future of Southern Protestantism may be more healthy than first meets the eye. Loss of establishment-status may be invigorating. The test will be whether white Southern churches can become more self-conscious as institutions and more theologically intentional, both essential if they are to play a decisive and sustaining role in the New South.

The greatest challenge for Southern churches, I think, will be to address the spiritual questions now being raised by the younger generations. As an older religious culture fades from the scene, many people will be increasingly unfamiliar with traditional religious language. Many boomers and Generation Xers already express dismay at much of the religious talk they hear. Perhaps for this reason, so many of them say that the "spiritual" is different from the "religious." To respond creatively to the situation, the churches will have to cultivate a special sensitivity for those born after World War II. What many of them are questing for today is a new coherence of faith and life, of body and spirit, of health and experience, of commitment and life. Southern Protestantism will be challenged to find ways to express the gospel in a discourse that resonates more to their changing world. It will have to be a discourse that accepts seeking as a religious enterprise, that respects the wisdom of experience, that acknowledges that truth might be found in many places and traditions, and that gives room for new styles of faith and practice.

To call for change, however, is not to abandon all continuity. Our task is to explore change in the context of continuity. I would go even further to suggest that Southern religion has certain cultural resources that may serve it well in the future. If in the century to come we face an emerging postmodern world with even further assaults upon tradition and fragmentation of life experiences, then the South's continuity with a cultural past may be of great importance—a buffer of sorts sheltering the impact of social change and serving as a basis for community. Briefly, let me comment on three possible resources in Southern culture:

One is the sense of place. If, indeed, a problem for the future is a sense of homelessness, or a metaphysical loss of place, then Southerners may experience less of it. For by contrast with the rest of the country, Southerners even in the New South have more of a grounding with place. Whether as found in novels or in the polls, Southerners seem to know whence they come and are more inclined to celebrate the ties of locality. Place, for Southerners, as Jean Heriot writes in her recent study of Southern religion, grounds the lives of Southerners "both in concrete reality and in shared cultural images."[20] As someone has said: Southerners often ask, "Where are you from?" Those above the Mason-Dixon Line ask, "What do you do?" Out West where I live they often ask, "What's your sign?"[21] Of the three, clearly the Southern question has more sustaining power.

Another resource is the sense of the tragic. Southerners have known defeat and struggle in ways that other Americans have not. That is not just a sentimental way of legitimating a history of racism, but to emphasize that concrete reality and shared cultural image resonate with the deepest of spiritual truths. The South may have, as Marshall Frady says, a romance with the cross and a preoccupation with the suffering Jesus, but the point is it has not lost sight of either the cross or suffering. One can hardly say the same for today's prosperity theology, possibility thinking, or much of the self-indulgent spirituality of our time. But the temptation in the South, of course, will be to go the way of the fleshpots,

---

[20]M. Jean Heriot, *Blessed Assurance: Beliefs, Actions, and the Experiences of Salvation in a Carolina Baptist Church* (Knoxville: University of Tennessee Press, 1994) 51.

[21]I am indebted to John Shelton Reed for this. See his *One South: An Ethnic Approach to Regional Culture*, 182.

to put its trust in progress and prosperity, and in so doing possibly lose this sense of the tragic.

Finally, there is the resource of lived experience. By lived experience, I mean that Southerners still have a capacity to encounter transcendence within ordinary experience. Everyday life in this part of the world is still endowed with a sense of the sacred in a way that might help to resist the powerful privatizing and secular trends of the larger culture. Strong religion is not that which is encapsulated in dry doctrine or creed, but that which arises out of life. The challenge ahead for the churches will be to find ways of leading people to new levels of social and spiritual consciousness without losing the common touch. And that will not be easy.

On Being a Christian
and a Southerner
at the Same Time ─────────

William H. Willimon

Things were tense on the Mercer University Campus. A scant four years
before, the Baptist College had racially integrated. Now, in 1968, blacks
were gaining the strength to challenge Mercer's campus mores. A particular source of contention was Kappa Alpha fraternity and its allegiance
to memories of the Confederate South. The KAs' "Old South Ball" was
enough of an affront to Mercer's black students. To top that insult, the
KAs had another tradition. With the KA brothers dressed in confederate
uniforms, their dates in hooped skirts of the 1860s, they marched in
double file to the women's dorm. There, swords were drawn, forming
arches of steel and in the name of 1860, as a brother would stand on the
steps with his costumed date, a solemn voice would announce, "Colonel
Jeb Stuart and his lady Flora," and so on.

On this night, a group of costumed black students meant to make a
mockery of the KAs' solemn rites. After several couples had been
announced, a black couple jumped in line and in a minstrel-like voice
announced, "Mr. Rastus Jones and his lady, Mandy." Then they would
prance through the crossed swords. Then, after a few more KA couples,
another couple jumped in line as a voice from the bushes called out, "Mr.
Bones and his lady, Minerva."

The dean of students at Mercer, watching on the sidelines, knew that
violence was going to be inescapable between a gathering throng of black
and white student taunters and the increasingly furious KAs. Sure
enough, the two groups began exchanging threats as they formed
themselves into two swarms of angry students glaring at one another
across an abyss of three hundred years of Southern history.

A black student jerked a small rebel flag of stars and bars from his pocket. The KAs knew what he was about to do--torch the symbol of the Confederacy.

Then recalls the dean, there was an awkward fumbling among the black students as they frantically searched for matches. Everything about their protest had been planned, it seemed, except for how to ignite the flag. Nobody had a match.

From out of the furious KAs, one fully uniformed Confederate stepped forth and stood before the black students, his comrades solidly aligned behind him. In the darkness, there was a gasp as they watched the KA pull from his pocket a long silver thing, glistening in the dark. There was a click, like that of a switchblade. A gasp. Then the faces of each group were illuminated by the KA's cigarette lighter.

"Hey, it's a piece of cloth," he said. And both astonished groups stood and watched the icon of the Lost Cause cringe, curl, and char.

Collegiate mayhem prevailed over violence, and both groups dispersed good naturedly to pursue their respective Saturday frivolities.[1]

This is a story of my people, black and white, who have been fated together in the South. If you don't like this story, if you find no revelation in it, then you are probably from Minnesota, in which case I worry that you may not find revelation in anything.

When asked to explain myself, I always say, "I'm from South Carolina," thinking that explains everything. I am marked, you see, indelibly stamped by a place and a history. To be from South Carolina, is to be special. Flannery O'Connor complained that "people from the North are not from anywhere." I'm from Greenville. My people have lived on the same land there since the mid-1700s. I'm from Greenville. There, fellow Greenvillians participated in and then tried to forget the last lynching of the modern era, the killing of Willie Earle in 1947. Because I no longer live on that land in Greenville, I now know what Flannery O'Connor meant when she complained, "The Anguish that most of us have observed for some time now has been caused not by the fact that the South is alienated from the rest of the country, but by the fact that it is not alienated enough, that everyday we are getting more and more like

[1]Will D. Campbell, *The Stem of Jesse: The Costs of Community at a 1960s Southern School* (Macon GA: Mercer University Press, 1995) 182-86.

the rest of the country, that we are being forced out, not only of our many sins but of our few virtues."[2]

My mother was from North Dakota, so she was for many years on probation in my father's family. My family tells the story of the time when my sister was invited to travel to Columbia for the day to see the governor's mansion, the statehouse, and all the sites.

When my sister returned home late that evening, my mother asked, "How was your trip with Grandmother to Columbia?"

My sister's lip began to tremble. She threw herself down on the sofa in tears.

"What went wrong?" my mother asked in alarm.

"Grandmother took me down to Columbia. We drove up to the Capitol. She pointed to two stars on the side of the building [the stars marking where Sherman's cannon balls struck] and said, 'See what your mother's people tried to do to our statehouse!' "

I tell my story, as a Southerner, in homage to the culture that marked me, a culture that may be passing, or which may be merely metamorphosing into a different form with which to effect the dominant culture. I don't know. I do know that, being a Southerner, I'm special.

I identify myself as a Southerner as a protest against the liberal fiction so prevalent in contemporary America--that it is possible to choose my story, that my identity is my own self-conscious construction, and that I am free to pick and choose who I will be from a variety of narrative options. I choose, therefore, I am.

Of course, the irony is that this fiction (I have no story other than that which I have personally chosen) is also a story, a result of the Cartesian, Kantian myth that I am most fully human when I have freely chosen who I want to be. This Enlightenment story is now being discredited by the simple observation that modern Americans have not chosen to live under the domination of the story that we have no story other than that which we have personally chosen. We were fated by a liberal culture that tends to exclude other accounts of who we are save

---

[2]Quoted by Stanley Hauerwas in "A Tale of Two Stories: On Being a Christian and a Texan," in *Christian Existence Today: Essays on Church, World, and Living in Between* (Durham NC: The Labyrinth Press, 1988) 25-45. I am indebted to Hauerwas for the form and the general theological claims of this essay.

the socially sanctioned, officially indoctrinated story that we have no story other than that which we have personally chosen.

The nice thing about being born in South Carolina is you could never believe such Kantian foolishness. I am formed by a story I did not choose. At no point can you peel away my history or natal geography and still have me. This is not a role I have chosen. It is my fate. Therefore much of my adult life, I realize belatedly, has been an effort to turn my fate into some sort of destiny. Is that not also true of other fateful aspects of us like male, female, white, black?

Yet for contemporary Americans, freedom means throwing off the limits of our birth, overcoming our history, and being rid of our parents. In our better moments, those of us from South Carolina know this effort to be futile. Like Faulkner's Quentin Compson in *Absalom! Absalom!* we find that, even at Harvard, we "can never be rid of the ghosts."

I recall, as a student at Yale during the dark days of the Viet Nam war, my first encounters with American innocence. There I met Midwesterners who had been opposed to the Viet Nam war since kindergarten, folk who claimed to have demonstrated against the war while still in preschool. There the hands were incredibly clean, their consciences wonderfully clear.

On the other hand, I had felt that the war was a good idea, at first. Here we were, the strong helping the weak, just like the missionaries. Later, I decided we were wrong. But here were folk who had never been wrong, not even in the backseat of a Chevrolet in high school.

I remember being taken aside by a brilliant fellow student from North Carolina (later a great attorney for the NAACP) who explained to me, "You don't need to get this thing right. You know your hands are dirty. You know you were conceived in sin. You're a Southerner." Then he added, "You'll never meet a Southerner who doesn't believe in original sin."

Which reminds me that I am not only living out the story of being a Southerner, I am also living out the story of being a Christian. And, as Christians we are told that freedom comes, not in denying our history, forgetting or overcoming it. Rather, our redemption is (in Stanley Hauerwas's words) "by being formed by a truthful narrative that helps us appreciate the limits and possibilities of those stories we have not chosen but are part and parcel of who we are."[3]

Everybody, even people from Nebraska, is story bound. It may be the KA-created myth of the Lost Cause; it may be the miserable myth of American innocence. The question is not, Will some story have its way with me? Rather it is, Which story is truthful enough to enable me to go on, despite being a Southerner?

Being a Southerner means that I am inextricably tied to that part of the United States that Reinhold Niebuhr once said was the only part of the country to have had "a significant history." That is, we were the only part of the country to have been, and to remain, dirt poor. Even into the present New South prosperity, we remain behind the North, economically. We were the only part of the country to have (before Viet Nam) lost a war and the only section to have endured a military occupation. All of this, said Niebuhr, ought to give the South an edge in battle with what was for Niebuhr the worst of the American demons, the demon of national innocence. A Southerner can be many things, but he or she ought not to be innocent--too many bodies, too much blood for that. I remember the day I discovered a crumpled paper at the bottom of a desk drawer, a certificate written in elegant, antique hand, "Received from W. H. Willimon, fifty dollars for one Negro female."

A few years ago, teaching in Germany, I was asked by my German faculty hosts, "Dr. Willimon, why have you invested so much time and effort in learning German and working with us here? Are you so interested in German theological scholarship?"

I responded, "Well, I'm from South Carolina. We got caught red handed, participating in a vast social evil; you got caught in evil. Of course, being Southerners, we were not as efficient in our slavery as you were in your genocide, but we have much in common."

Such a regional story ought to give a person an edge against the self-righteous, arrogant, and ultimately, deadly naiveté' which has so characterized this country's national history. Alas, it was a Southerner who mired us in Viet Nam. (Johnson was a Texan, at least.) But then again it was a Southerner who stood on the steps of the Lincoln Memorial and skillfully manipulated our national innocence into a weapon set against

---

[3]Hauerwas, "A Tale of Two Stories," 29.

our ugly national secret. It was a Southerner who turned our nightmare of racism into a dream of racial harmony. What makes the difference between our turning the Civil War into the myth of the Lost Cause and our bold willingness to tell the truth about ourselves, even when the truth is as painful as the truth about South Carolina?

I entered Wofford College as the first class to include an African American (1964). Yet, in the year of my graduation (1968), our eyes turned all too briefly toward Orangeburg where six students were gunned down (most shot in the back) by the South Carolina highway patrol.[4] Today, the nation celebrates the Civil Rights movement as an image of us at our best. Few remember the Orangeburg massacre. Why? Is it that we lack a story that enables us to tell the truth?

One reason why America finds it so tough to tell the truth is that we find it impossible to acknowledge any evil that we can't set right.[5] But there are some things—like my great grandfather's dabbling in slavery or the Orangeburg massacre—that can't be set right, cannot be made up for. So we deny the evil and thus become more dangerous to ourselves and our neighbors in our violent attempt to preserve our righteousness. In denying the tragedy in the story of being a Southerner, I never develop the skills necessary to free myself from my self-deceit. In the South in the sixties, we almost destroyed ourselves, almost, by defending the Southern story as if that story were the central story of our lives, denying the tragedy, defending our denial with murderous intensity.

It's tough for Americans to be honest about the tragic. Surely this is one reason why we continue to have difficulty with the integration of African Americans into the dominant culture.

African Americans, through no choice of their own, bear with them a history that is incompatible with American myths of who we wish to God we were. The very presence of black people is a visible reminder that we have been, and still are, other than decent. So we must pervert the story. Look how we have transformed an angry, disillusioned-with-liberals Martin Luther King, Jr., into a celebrated icon of ourselves at our best. How shall we ever tell the truth?

---

[4]See Jack Bass and Jack Nelson, *The Orangeburg Massacre* (Macon GA: Mercer University Press, 1984).

[5]The thought is Hauerwas's, "A Tale of Two Stories," 38.

It is the claim of the baptized that, only as my story is grasped by the more truthful story of the Christ, do I finally receive the resources to tell my story in a way that does not deny the tragic in my story. Christians are Christians, in great part, because they have listened to a certain story. That story of the way God intruded among us, taking our fate unto himself, even unto a cross, enables me to be a Southerner without hating myself or my neighbor for my being caught in such a story. It is a story about a God who came to us, only to be nailed by us, a story so foreign to our illusions of goodness. It is a story about God's willingness to forget and not hold our sin against us. The sin is not downplayed or denied in the story of the cross, yet neither is sin granted ultimate power over our lives.

So Will Campbell, in telling his story of the KAs and their black defiers at Mercer, speaks of repentance as the first essential step toward mending the enmity between black and white. Campbell speaks as a Christian. You cannot know what he means by a weird word like "repentance" unless you let him tell you a story. And he will, if you'll sit for it. A story about a group of young college kids, squared off in the darkness, ready to repeat the same script enacted by their grandfathers. Yet not this night, in the glow of a good natured gesture, relativizing, transmogrifying history into redemption. A story illumined by another grander, more difficult, more enlightening story even than that of being from South Carolina, the story of a God who, though whipped and lynched, looked down at us and in a good natured gesture, whispered, "Sisters and brothers, I love you still."

One Denomination, Many Centers: The Southern Baptist Situation—

Bill Leonard

The Cooperative Baptist Fellowship, the Alliance of Baptists, Baptists Committed, the Conservative Baptist Fellowship, Baptist Theological Seminary at Richmond (Virginia), George W. Truett Theological Seminary, Mid-America Baptist Seminary, Gardner-Webb Theology School, Beeson Divinity School, Baptist Center for Ethics, Smyth & Helwys Publishing, Associated Baptist Press, and *Baptists Today*. That list, far from exhaustive, is but a brief sample of the ever expanding network of organizations related in some way to something called the Southern Baptist Convention (hereafter SBC), the largest Protestant denomination in America. Most, though not all, of these groups were established by persons linked to the so-called moderate contingent of the SBC—individuals and churches who lost in a fifteen-year political and theological struggle to control the denomination. While that convention-wide conflict has created significant fragmentation, as yet no formal schism has occurred. In fact, these new organizations are supported by congregations and individuals who continue to retain some type of Southern Baptist identity and affiliation.

From its beginning in 1845 the SBC established a powerful sense of denominational loyalty among its adherents, utilizing programmatical, cultural, and theological forces to unite varying regional, local, and ideological subgroups. The connectionalism created by the convention held within it both the seeds of unity and disunity. On one hand, the denomination formed an identifiable religious and organizational center, uniting a surprisingly diverse constituency in common education, publication, missionary, and other benevolent endeavors. As inevitable cultural and denominational transitions occurred, however, the constituency, hopelessly divided over theology and polity, established numerous centers of ecclesiastical life, each in varying ways continuing to claim or cling to fragments of the Southern Baptist mantle.

The Loss of the Center

The structure of the national denomination, now solidly under fundamentalist control, continues to maintain traditional agencies and institutions, appealing for support to customary allegiances among its members. While many remain supportive of such denominational enterprises, others across the theological spectrum seem less invested in promoting and underwriting "the Program." Although they dominate the national bureaucracy, fundamentalist leaders seem unable either to recreate a new denominational center that will unite the fundamentalist majority or to articulate a strategy for dealing with the recalcitrant moderate minority. As they lose the financial and programmatic support of moderates, fundamentalists also face declining denominational loyalty on the part of their own constituents.

While SBC moderates are increasingly hesitant to sustain traditional programs and funding mechanisms, many are also unwilling to break completely with the mother denomination. While persons and churches across the theological spectrum continue to claim the name Southern Baptist, their Baptist identity is nurtured less by participation in the national denomination than through a variety of subgroups inside and outside the convention. The Southern Baptist Convention, therefore, remains a huge denominational bureaucracy, but with new centers of energy and organization evident at almost every level of the traditional Southern Baptist system. Historic loyalties remain so deep and powerful, however, that even those most opposed to present fundamentalist agendas still maintain a stubborn reluctance to relinquish either the name Southern Baptist or official membership in the denomination itself.

Fifteen years have passed since, in 1979, SBC fundamentalists first elected Adrian Rogers, pastor of Bellevue Baptist Church, Memphis, as president of the convention. Since that time, Rogers and a succession of like-minded presidents have overseen the appointment of fundamentalist trustees to all convention-owned agencies and institutions. In short, fundamentalists now control those national entities including six seminaries, the huge Sunday School Board publishing house, the Home and Foreign

Missions Boards, the Christian Life Commission, Annuity Board, Educational and Historical Commissions, and the Executive Committee, that assembly charged with the day-to-day administration of the convention.

These agencies reflect the connectionalism of the convention system established with the founding of the denomination in 1845. That system created a more intricate relationship between churches and denominational organizations than had the older society structure that characterized earlier Baptist cooperative endeavors. The convention plan united multiple agencies and ministries around a single center—the Southern Baptist Convention. The society, on the other hand, was an autonomous confederation of individuals, churches, and regional associations focused on an exclusive benevolent task related to missions, publication, education, or evangelism.

As the SBC controversy and certain transitions in American denominational life have impacted the system, however, Southern Baptists seem to be returning to particular forms of the society method. Indeed, a certain implicit societization is evident throughout SBC life, creating innumerable centers of ideology and action. That new reality may be illustrated through a survey of various organizational, educational, regional, and local transitions in SBC life.

Before turning to those changes, it is important to offer one more clarification. The movement away from the denominational center is characteristic of Southern Baptists across the theological and political spectrum. While recent history has given evidence of new organizations founded by those of the moderate faction, the fundamentalist bloc was among the first denominational subgroups to found new educational institutions, to develop alternative funding mechanisms, and to look beyond the SBC for teaching materials and missionary opportunities.

As the controversy evolved, fundamentalists and moderates reversed roles. Early on, fundamentalists were unapologetically critical of the denominational system, while moderates upheld the tradition. Fundamentalists now call for unyielding denominational loyalty, while moderates are generating their own societies for service and mission. How long these groups can remain part of the Southern Baptist family is impossible to estimate.

Organizational Centers

The move away from the denomination as center is evident in the growth of new organizational structures among Southern Baptists. This phenomenon first became apparent in the actions of SBC fundamentalists during the 1970s and 80s. Frustrated because of their limited voice in shaping convention policies and actions, fundamentalists often "designated" funds toward or away from specific convention agencies. Some fundamentalist congregations reduced their support of the Cooperative Program, the denomination's corporate funding mechanism. They also supported a variety of new programs and institutions that were outside official SBC structures but were aimed at Southern Baptist constituents.

When the six Southern Baptist seminaries seemed too liberal or insensitive to fundamentalist concerns, three new schools (two seminaries and one college) were established. The seminaries were Mid-America Baptist Seminary, Memphis, founded in 1971, and Luther Rice Seminary, originally founded in Florida in 1961 and now in Atlanta. Although neither receives SBC funds directly, both claim Southern Baptist identity. Both are staffed by Southern Baptist professors and educate persons for ministry among Southern Baptists.

When fundamentalists felt that their views were not presented in the state Baptist periodicals, they formed their own publications, the *Southern Baptist Journal* and the *Southern Baptist Advocate*. These newspapers contained fundamentalist critiques of the denominational system, exposed liberalism in denominationally funded institutions, and made direct attacks on convention employees, particularly seminary and university professors. These actions directed energy and identity away from the denominational center. Try as they might, the leadership of the SBC during those turbulent years (from 1979 forward) could not refocus denominational unity on common missionary or evangelical endeavors.

As fundamentalists gained increasing control of the national denomination, SBC moderates also initiated new organizations and networks. One of the earliest such entities was the Southern Baptist Alliance (now the Alliance of Baptists) begun in 1986. It originated as a specific reaction to increasing fundamentalist dominance in convention life. The statement of purpose declared:

The Southern Baptist Alliance is an alliance of individuals and churches dedicated to the preservation of historic Baptist principles, freedoms, and traditions and the continuance of our ministry and mission within the Southern Baptist Convention.

Princeton Seminary professor Alan Neely writes that the last phrase regarding the SBC "was a calculated addition," not acceptable to all involved in the new group. Yet, he continues, "It was accepted as a practical necessity in order to avoid being regarded as a splinter group bent on leading people and congregations out of the SBC." By 1991 that phrase was "quietly dropped" from the statement of purpose, and in 1992 the Southern Baptist Alliance became the Alliance of Baptists.

This change of name identifies a group of individuals and churches that cooperate together in mission and reach out to Baptists of various stripes. Most "Alliance churches" continue to maintain some affiliation with the SBC, however. With offices and executive director based in Washington, DC, the Alliance represents the most progressive (some would say liberal) organization in the moderate wing of the SBC. It funds various projects including mission activities, occasional publications, and different education projects.

The Cooperative Baptist Fellowship (hereafter CBF) is perhaps the best known new organization of moderates. Founded in 1991,[1] its earliest formal statements declared that these moderates were not leaving the SBC but simply redirecting their energies toward more positive endeavors. One document noted that,

A denomination is a missions delivery system; it is not meant to be an idol. When we make more of the SBC than we ought, we risk falling into idolatry. Twelve years is too long to engage in political activity. We are called to higher purposes.

These articles detailed the purpose of the CBF in terms of missions, funding, and giving "energies to the advancement of the Kingdom of God rather than in divisive, destructive politics." All this did not require that

---

[1]A precursory meeting was held in Atlanta in 1990. Formal organization occurred in 1991.

these Baptists "severe ties with the old Southern Baptist Convention."
Rather, they suggested,

> It does give us another mission delivery system, one more like our
> understanding of what it means to be Baptist and what it means to do
> gospel. Therefore, we create a new instrument to further the Kingdom
> and enlarge the Body of Christ.

The CBF has developed rapidly with substantial budget increases
over the last three years. It now receives more than fourteen million
dollars annually from Southern Baptist individuals and churches. With
offices in Atlanta, the CBF now funds its own missionaries, contributes
to the support of several new seminaries, provides scholarships for
Baptist ministerial students, and offers a variety of services for Southern
Baptist congregations.

An increasing number of Southern Baptist churches now permit
members to designate their offerings for traditional SBC programs or the
CBF. While this approach is evident only among a minority of the 35,000
SBC churches, fundamentalists have shown tremendous concern about
such defections. At the SBC annual meeting in 1994, the convention
voted to reject all monies that came directly from the CBF. Until then,
the CBF offered several funding plans, one of which allowed traditional
support for SBC agencies. Contributions were sent through the CBF
offices in Atlanta rather than denominational headquarters in Nashville,
however. The convention's rejection of those funds led to the end of that
option from the CBF. CBF supporters have also formed state organizations that foster various regional programs, further expanding the
decentralization of SBC-related churches.

One question remains unanswered. How long can the Cooperative
Baptist Fellowship maintain its shadow relationship with the Southern
Baptist Convention? Many fundamentalists insist that the CBF has all the
characteristics of a denomination and should declare itself as such, offering Baptists a choice between one denominational organization or the
other. Many inside and outside the CBF wonder if and when the movement should become a denomination. At this time, leaders seem willing
to wait before making any definitive declaration or burning bridges ir-
revocably with the SBC. The truth is, CBF leaders recognize that few of
their constituents are willing, even now, to break all ties with the SBC.

They seem content, for the present, to remain officially in the SBC, offering options for both those nonfundamentalists who prefer the traditional mechanisms of the denomination and those who do not.

The CBF is not the only new movement under development, however. A variety of special-service organizations have also appeared among SBC moderates. One of the most successful is Smyth & Helwys Publishing, Inc., based in Macon, Georgia. Established in 1990, the company markets books and teaching materials primarily for a Southern Baptist audience. The initial statement of purpose read:

> The purpose of Smyth & Helwys is to offer supplemental and alternative materials for Baptists who have become increasingly concerned about the future direction of the Convention Press and Broadman [SBC publishing houses]. . . . Those involved in the formation of Smyth & Helwys feel it is time for a press committed to freedom of inquiry and reverent biblical scholarship, but which is at the same time autonomous and therefore free from denominational controversy.

The publishers soon established a new Bible Study curriculum known as "Formations" for use in Baptist churches. They recently projected publication of a commentary series for moderate Southern Baptists and other evangelicals. In only four years the corporation has expanded rapidly, recently completing construction of a new office building in Macon. Smyth & Helwys is a completely autonomous organization with no direct ties to CBF or any other Baptist body. Clearly, its constituency parallels that of the CBF. It represents another society-type association alongside the SBC.

It may also be noted that the Smyth & Helwys "Formations" Sunday School material is only one alternative curriculum now used by churches associated with the SBC. During the last decade Southern Baptist churches have expanded their use of Sunday School curriculum beyond the denomination's Sunday School Board. Sales at that agency have declined as churches have looked to other sources, from the conservative publisher David C. Cook to Smyth & Helwys' "Formations" to American Baptist and other mainline denominational publishing houses.

Educational Institutions

The establishment of Baptist organizations is also evident in the rapid expansion of new educational institutions for ministerial students aimed primarily at a Baptist constituency. Indeed, the proliferation of Baptist seminaries and divinity schools has been so extensive that Daniel Aleshire, vice president of the Association of Theological Schools (ATS) recently noted that since World War II Baptists have founded more seminaries than any other denomination.

The Southern Baptist Convention currently funds six theological seminaries spread across the country from Wake Forest, North Carolina, to San Francisco, California. While these schools have been at the center of numerous denominational controversies throughout the convention's history, they have also facilitated an extensive network of denominational education and placement.

As already noted, fundamentalist dissatisfaction with the SBC seminaries, led to the founding of additional Baptist seminaries. These included Mid-America Baptist Theological Seminary and Luther Rice Seminary. The latter school developed an extensive curriculum by correspondence, offering its own—marginally accredited—masters and doctors degrees. Criswell College, founded by W. A. Criswell, longtime fundamentalist pastor of First Baptist Church, Dallas, Texas, offers Bible School degrees to Baptist ministers. These institutions continue to train Southern Baptist ministers and missionaries. They have created their own networks of SBC fundamentalists.

As the six SBC seminaries came under the control of fundamentalists, SBC moderates moved to establish new educational institutions for ministerial training. The first of these was Baptist Theological Seminary at Richmond, Virginia, founded in 1991. That school receives no SBC funds but does obtain money from both the Alliance of Baptists and the Cooperative Baptist Fellowship, as well as from a variety of SBC-affiliated congregations and individuals.

By 1994, numerous theological institutions had been founded or were scheduled to begin operation by the year two thousand. Those already underway include Gardner-Webb School of Theology, Gardner-Webb University, Boiling Springs, North Carolina; George W. Truett Theological Seminary, Baylor University, Waco, Texas; Hardin-Simmons School of Theology, Hardin-Simmons University, Abilene, Texas; and

Beeson Divinity School, Samford University, Birmingham, Alabama. Although the latter school was not founded specifically in response to the SBC controversy, and the donor bequest mandates a more ecumenical faculty and student body, its primary constituency comes from Southern Baptists. Mercer University, Macon, Georgia, and Wake Forest University, Winston-Salem, North Carolina, have indicated plans to established new divinity schools but only when proper funding can be secured.[2] In response to fundamentalists' dismissal of Russell Dilday as president of Southwestern Baptist Theological Seminary, Fort Worth, a group of Texas Baptists are studying the feasibility for a consortium of theological centers across the state. Baptist seminaries, like Spring, are bustin' out all over.

At the same time, an increasing number of Southern Baptist students are discovering the broader world of theological education outside Southern Baptist institutions. Both Duke University Divinity School and Candler School of Theology, Emory University, have established Baptist Houses that offer specific courses and identity to Baptist students at those institutions. Other seminaries and divinity schools are discovering that the Southern Baptist market is fertile ground. Many offer scholarships that make them competitive with the six SBC seminaries.

Transitions in the nature of theological education for Southern Baptist ministers have significant implications for ministerial identity and Baptist denominational consciousness. In the past, the vast majority of SBC ministers were educated in the massive seminary system. These schools not only inculcated a powerful denominational identity into their students, but their alumni support system linked graduates with the larger denominational network promoting SBC programs, publications, missions methods, and ministerial placement. Seminaries helped maneuver ministers into the corporate system of the SBC. Now the pipelines to the six seminaries are drying up or being redirected. Newer schools are more regionally oriented or exist outside the denomination entirely. Clearly, the next generation of Southern Baptist ministers will have a different identity than their predecessors, whatever their choice of a seminary or

---

[2][Editors' note: Subsequent to the the delivery of this address by Leonard, Mercer and Wake Forest finalized plans for their theological schools. The Mercer Shool of Theology is to open in the fall of 1996 in Atlanta, Georgia. The Wake Forest Divinity School, with Bill Leonard as its dean, is to begin offering classes no later than 2000.]

divinity school. Churches must learn to ask new questions and explore new resources for securing ministers, all of which has major implications for denominational organization and identity.

Regional Transitions

Equally important to denominational life are the changes now taking place regionally throughout the SBC system. This is particularly evident in the changing relationships between the national SBC and the individual state conventions.

Concerning the connection between the national convention and state Baptist conventions, the SBC constitution reads:

> While independent and sovereign in its own sphere, the Convention does not claim and will never attempt to exercise any authority over any other Baptist body, whether church, auxiliary organizations, association or convention.

In the Southern Baptist system, state conventions are autonomous bodies that originally provided special programs, agencies, and institutions for Baptists in those southern states that formed the convention. By the 1950s, as Southern Baptists expanded throughout the nation, additional state conventions were established. These conventions hold their own annual meetings, usually in the fall, electing officers who appoint nominating committees for trustee boards controlled by the state denomination. Historically these state-funded agencies included Baptist hospitals, children's home, mission programs, and state Baptist colleges and universities. In the denominational system, seminaries were owned and operated by the national denomination, while colleges were controlled by the states. With the establishment of the Cooperative Program of collective denominational funding in 1925, Southern Baptist churches in each state forwarded their denominational monies to the state conventions, which then sent a portion of those funds to the national body, retaining the rest for state-run operations. While states were autonomous, they were closely linked to national SBC programs, funds, and identity. Those relationships are now being renegotiated, particularly from the perspective of the states.

Marse Grant, moderate editor emeritus of the *Biblical Recorder*, the Baptist paper in North Carolina, wrote recently that,

Baptist state conventions finally are exercising their autonomy so effectively that Nashville and its obedient entities understand what's happening. States are taking seriously the protection given them by Article IV (in the SBC constitution). . . . No longer do states believe that it's 'traditional' for them to send their money to the (SBC) executive committee with few or no questions asked.

As the controversy extends throughout denominational life, state conventions are reexamining their connections to the national denomination. For example, the Baptist General Convention of Texas, the SBC's largest state organization, recently approved a redefinition of Cooperative Program funding for member churches. In the new plan, congregations will be considered "cooperating churches" (participants in the Cooperative Program) if they contribute to the traditional Cooperative Program system, if they give money only to Texas Baptist programs, or choose to designate funds to other mission efforts such as the Baptist World Alliance, the Baptist Joint Committee on Public Affairs, or the Cooperative Baptist Fellowship. This plan represents a new definition of what it means to be a Southern Baptist church, expanding connections and identity toward multiple Baptist entities, related or unrelated to the national denomination. In response to these actions Morris Chapman, fundamentalist president of the SBC executive committee, declared that the plan is "a departure from the partnership which has long existed between the state convention and the SBC." The Texas plan could essentially turn the state convention into its own regional denomination linked financially to varying Baptist entities inside and outside the old SBC.

Texas is not alone in redefining its SBC connections. North Carolina Baptists can now select alternative funding procedures that permit reallocation of money to and away from fundamentalist or moderate programs. Virginia churches may choose one of three plans which allow traditional SBC contributions, funding CBF alone, and a combination of the two. All this suggests that states are asserting their autonomy and providing constituents with multiple choices in order not to alienate large numbers of persons or congregations in their particular region. Virginia fundamentalists have founded their own organization, Southern Baptist Conservatives of Virginia, channeling funds directly to it and away from the state Baptist convention.

At the same time, traditionally state-operated institutions such as hospitals and universities are renegotiating their relationship with their respective conventions. Hospitals were among the first to distance themselves from the parent Baptist bodies. Often this involved a mutual agreement born of the state convention's fear of ascending liability for malpractice or other cases against Baptist hospitals. More public and poignant, perhaps, has been the decision of numerous colleges and universities to redefine relationships with the Baptist conventions that owned and operated them.

There are more than sixty Southern Baptist colleges and universities across the U.S., most related directly to the Baptist conventions in their particular states. Many were founded in the nineteenth century, originally with self-perpetuating boards of trustees. Over time these colleges were united with state conventions that provided substantial funding and appointed trustees. During the last two decades, however, some of the best known Southern Baptist institutions of higher education have claimed greater autonomy, redefining their ties with the state Baptist conventions. Schools such as the University of Richmond (Virginia) and Wake Forest University (North Carolina) were among the first universities to change their status. As their endowments increased and student bodies diversified, these schools concluded that the control by the Baptist state convention was no longer to their advantage. These concerns were exacerbated as the controversy between moderates and fundamentalists extended throughout the SBC, made particularly poignant in the turmoil that beset trustee boards in several of the seminaries. Since 1990, a number of Baptist-affiliated institutions have modified charters and by-laws to allow boards of trustees to become self-perpetuating. These include Furman University, Greenville, South Carolina; Baylor University, Waco, Texas; Stetson University, DeLand, Florida; and, most recently, Samford University, Birmingham, Alabama; and Mississippi College, Clinton, Mississippi. In another arrangement, the North Carolina Baptist Convention approved a plan whereby Baptist colleges and universities in that state may appoint their own trustees in direct proportion to the amount of money they receive from the convention.

Recent trustee actions at Samford University illustrate the transition underway in many schools. Founded as Howard College in 1841, Samford's original trustee board was self-perpetuating. In 1845, the board amended its charter to permit trustees to be selected by the Alabama Baptist Convention, organized that same year. In 1994, trustees, by a

30–2 vote, returned appointment powers to the board itself. The board released the following rationale for the revisions:

> It appears that political factors increasingly impact the Southern Baptist Convention, with obvious potential to disrupt the Alabama Convention. These factors, along with proposals concerning denominational trustees here in Alabama, have raised the possibility that great harm could come to Samford. If the election of Samford trustees—who have ultimate responsibility for Samford University—is placed in doubt every year, and the threat of "stacking" the Board of Trustees with persons of particular political loyalties is ever-present, and Samford is regularly harassed with minor charges only to be exploited for what appear to be political objectives, then the University's current operations and future progress are jeopardized.

Trustees will continue to be chosen only from Alabama Baptist churches. The university will maintain its Christian orientation within a Baptist perspective. The action, trustees noted, was "intended to protect Samford from the future ebb and flow of denominational politics." In short, the trustees simply returned their selection process to that of a private institution, or society, with fraternal, though not appointive, relationship with the Alabama Baptist Convention.

Barely a week after the Samford action, the trustees of yet another Baptist institution, Mississippi College, took a similar action. Trustees of that school released a statement noting that the action was taken "to ensure that Mississippi College can remain true to its Baptist heritage and tradition of serving all Mississippi Baptists and their churches by distancing the College from denominational politics."

These two Baptists institutions are simply the latest in a growing number of Baptist-related colleges and universities that are redefining their relationship to their respective state conventions. While issues of politics, finances, and institutional stability are evident in each case, the changes also have the effect of creating new, autonomous centers of Baptist educational and ecclesial identity.

Local Issues

The movement away from the denominational center is nowhere more evident than transitions taking place at the local level among Southern

Baptist congregations. From the beginning of the Baptist tradition, the local church has been the basis of Baptist ecclesiology. Congregational polity was based on the belief that Christ was head of the church, his authority mediated through the local communion. Early Baptists mistrusted organizational entanglements that might undermine the authority and centrality of the specific congregation. One of the great achievements of the SBC denomination builders was their ability to create a strong sense of loyalty in such a fiercely independent people. Such identity was not easily achieved and not without controversies over missions, Sunday Schools, cooperative giving, and other expressions of collaborate endeavor. Yet by the 1950s, and probably well before, Southern Baptist churches understood themselves in and through the national and state conventions. They utilized educational materials through the Sunday School Board, sent messengers to the annual meetings, contributed to the Cooperative Program, called ministers educated at Baptist colleges and seminaries, and understood their primary religious identity as Southern Baptists. All that is changing.

As with other mainline denominations, intermarriage and enlistment programs have brought persons to SBC churches who have neither the familial nor cultural background of Southern Baptistness. Local and regional considerations have led many churches to keep more of their money at home. The continuing controversy has created divisions in local congregations, many of which are forced to declare themselves as to their position in the denominational conflict. Some estimates suggest that some 120 Southern Baptist ministers are terminated from their church positions every month. While most churches continue to allow members only to contribute to traditional Cooperative Program funding, a growing number —many of them significant congregations in their respective regions— permit multiple possibilities in the distribution of funds. As already noted, churches across the theological and political spectrum now utilize a variety of educational and resource materials, many of which are not published by the SBC. Fundamentalists and moderates alike acknowledge that the old denominational loyalties are more evident among persons over forty while the younger generation of Southern Baptists are less likely to follow the traditional denominational line, whatever their theological orientation.

This is particularly evident among those influenced by the so- called megachurch movement, now rapidly affecting Southern Baptist life.

Megachurch methods are setting agendas for congregations across the SBC. A megachurch may be defined as a congregation of several thousand members, dispensing specialized services targeted for specific subgroups, usually led by a charismatic authority-figure pastor, and organized around distinct marketing techniques. Megachurches are essentially mini-denominations, offering in one congregation many activities previously administered through the larger denominational system. Many of these churches minimize their denominational affiliation, publish their own educational materials, fund their own missions programs, and send a smaller percentage of their funds to the denominational enterprise. Younger ministers, both fundamentalist and moderate, influenced by megachurch trends, are less likely to expend their energy on denominational battles. Indeed, many speak of the death of denominations and the rise of new megachurch paradigms for ministry in the twenty-first century. Clearly, megachurches create new ecclesiastical centers that redirect energies toward local church-based ministry and away from traditional convention programs and policies. Their impact on Southern Baptists deserves extensive study and analysis.

Conclusions: Intentionality and Identity

Localism has also contributed to a growing sense of intentionality among SBC affiliated churches. With the decline of denominational consciousness and the fragmentation of denominational programs, many churches are confronting questions of identity. For example, what does it mean to be Baptist? What elements of the Baptist heritage should be retained and passed on to another generation?

In earlier, more denominationally conscious times, strategies for missions, evangelism, social ministry, and Baptist identity were articulated by the denomination. Churches simply ordered literature, adopted prescribed programs, and wrote checks for mission funding. As those old connections are changed or eliminated, churches must be more intentional as to their identity and purpose within the Baptist heritage. Many are reasserting the idea of the local church as the center of mission, learning, worship, and ministry, and are utilizing their resources to support ministry inside and outside traditional denominational programs.

At least in the short term, these transitions point to a return to the society method that characterized Baptists' first attempts at denominational cooperation. The society method was a way in which Baptists who did not trust "hierarchies" beyond the local church joined together in missionary and benevolent efforts that they could not accomplish on their own. Each society was itself autonomous, established to provide particular ministries in home or foreign missions, education, publication, or benevolence. Membership was extended to individuals, churches, and other Baptist associations. These organizations were clearing houses for ministry, bringing together persons of varying regions and theological persuasions in common action. Churches and individuals "shopped around" for those programs that particularly captured their energy and interest. Funding came from direct appeals to the constituency, not from a centralized denominational finance system. In fact, when the SBC was first created, "delegates" to its annual meetings included representatives of churches and associations as well as solitary individuals all of whom had made the necessary contributions to the work of the fledgling denomination.

At the present time Southern Baptists function on several levels of denominational identity and support. While the old system remains, engendering continued loyalty from large numbers of persons, new forms of cooperation, organization, and action are evident throughout SBC life. Theological disputes and political machinations have created a tremendous spirit of mistrust among and within the various regional and ideological subgroups which compose the convention. While a powerful sense of denominational identity lingers, particularly among those over the age of fifty, a growing number of Southern Baptists no longer think of their primary religious identity in terms of an exclusively denominational identity. Not only are regional and local associations reasserting their autonomy but new Baptist-supported agencies also are being established. A defacto society method is returning to the denomination. At every level of denominational life, questions arise as to what it means to be Baptist and how to pass on a Baptist identity to a new generation raised in the midst of controversy and transition. Those leaders—national, regional, and local—who refuse to confront these powerful realities, will find the future most unmanageable. For Southern Baptist moderates and fundamentalists alike, the twenty-first century may be a most difficult period for establishing a new denomination or maintaining an old one.

Emerging Challenges for Black Churches in the Twenty-first Century: With a Focus on the South as a Region

Lawrence H. Mamiya

Returning to South Carolina in particular brings back some fond memories of our many research trips to this state when Eric Lincoln and I were undertaking the historical and survey research of black churches throughout the country. One of the trips included an excursion to visit the Silver Bluff Baptist Church in South Carolina, a rural church still in existence that is regarded as one of the earliest, if not the earliest, black church in America. The church has claimed a much disputed founding date of 1750 on its cornerstone.[1] Lincoln and I also visited the churches among the Gullah people of the Sea Islands, particularly on the island of D'Aufuskie. We stopped at the famous Emmanuel A.M.E. Church in Charleston, where Denmark Vesey's courageous rebellion was planned in 1822. As I drove Eric's Mercedes on one of these trips, we were passing a swampy area of marshland when suddenly he shouted, "I can hear those voices! I can hear those voices! I can hear their screams!" I remember looking around the car and asking, "What voices?" Then I looked at Eric. His eyes were filled with tears, and he was sobbing

---

[1]Most historians tend to date the founding of the Silver Bluff Baptist Church about twenty-five years later, circa 1774–1776. See Carter G. Woodson, *History of the Negro Church*. Also see C. Eric Lincoln and Lawrence H. Mamiya, *The Black Church in the African American Experience*, (Durham NC: Duke University Press, 1990) for some background on this dispute about the earliest black churches.

uncontrollably. After he regained his composure, he explained that it was into swampy areas like this and into the many rivers and lakes of plantation country that the bodies of thousands of African slaves and later African Americans were thrown, after having been beaten, mutilated, tortured, and sometimes lynched. Whenever I write or speak about black churches, I am often reminded of that incident when one of the most famous scholars of black religion had the capacity to transcend time and space to feel and participate in the emotional pain of those anonymous Africans who were just called slaves. It has also taught me that we as scholars and students of religion, as historians, theologians, and sociologists, need to develop the sensitivity and capacity to hear the voices, cries, and screams and to share in the suffering of those whom we study. If we cannot do that, then where are we?

I tell this story partly because it occurred in South Carolina but more so because it is a reminder of the continuing importance of the racial factor in the study of American religion, as Dr. Willimon reiterated yesterday. Constant racial discrimination and brutalization of African Americans eventually led to the establishment of the seven historically independent black denominations among the Baptists, Methodists, and Pentecostals.[2] For more than two hundred years, the arena of religion has remained the most segregated area in American society and Sunday morning at 11 A.M. as the most segregated hour; the prospects are likely that the situation will remain so in the future unless American society changes drastically.

I tell this story to address the changes and trends that I see among the black denominations and churches that will affect the future of Protestantism in black communities, particularly in the South. I will address four challenges with which black churches are faced and consider how their response will affect their growth and stability. These challenges are: first, the growing class differentiation occurring in black communities nationally; second, the phenomenon of denominationalism and the rise of nondenominational megachurches and whether there are the loosening of

---

[2]The seven independent black denominations include: the National Baptist Convention, U.S.A.; the National Baptist Convention of America; the Progressive National Baptist Convention; the African Methodist Episcopal Church; the African Methodist Episcopal Zion Church; the Christian Methodist Episcopal Church; and the Church of God in Christ.

ties to denominations and a corresponding weakening of theological traditions; third, the Neopentecostal movement in some black denominations and the challenge of church growth; and fourth, the pluralistic challenge presented by the vibrant growth of Islam and other African-based religious traditions in black communities.

Before addressing these challenges, let me point out that, on the whole, the black denominations have not experienced the severe decline in church membership that several of the mainline white denominations have experienced in the past two decades, which has been estimated from one-third to more than fifty percent.[3] Clearly, the dynamics that have affected the decline in white church membership differ from that of black churches. For example, civil rights activism and participation in Vietnam protests, and support for liberal social programs by church leaders have aggravated white Christians at the grass roots level. The movement towards conservative and right-wing politics among many whites nationwide has been reflected in the growth of fundamentalism and conservative evangelicalism. Likewise, the bashing of federal and state government bureaucracy has found its counterpart in bashing church bureaucracies at the denominational levels, including the National Council and the World Council of Churches. While there has been some growth of conservative Republicanism among African Americans to about ten per cent of the voting electorate, the vast majority of black voters (90%) have supported liberal social policies and programs. Politically, most African Americans have tended to support federal government intervention and programs, a reflection of their experience with intransigent state governments during the civil rights period. Black churches and denominations still remain very strong social institutions in their communities, partly due to the paucity of alternative institutions. However, there are a number of challenges on the horizon that pose a threat to their stability and growth in the twenty-first century.

---

[3]For the data on the decline of the mainline denominations, see Dean R. Hoge and David A. Roozen, editors, *Understanding Church Growth and Decline: 1950–1978,* (New York: Pilgrim, 1979). Also see Wade Clark Roof and William McKinney, *American Mainline Religion: Its Changing Shape and Future,* (New Brunswick NJ: Rutgers University Press, 1987).

The Challenge of a Widening Class Gap: The Growth of the Black Poor

In our study, *The Black Church in the African American Experience*, we pointed out that the greatest challenge to the future of black churches concerns the growing gulf between the "coping" sector of middle-income, working-class, and middle-class black communities, on the one hand, and a "crisis" sector of poor black communities made up of the working poor and the dependent poor, on the other. The demographic movement of middle-income blacks out of inner city areas—and into residential parts of the cities, older suburbs, or into newly created black suburbs, has meant a growing physical and social isolation of the black poor.[4] For example, since the 1960s, forty eight percent of the black population of Atlanta has moved out of the central city into surrounding counties.[5] This social isolation of the poor has created crisis conditions, from high rates of black-on-black crime and teen pregnancy to growing drug use and widespread unemployment, in urban black ghettos. The gradual emergence of two fairly distinct black Americas along class lines—of two nations within a nation—has raised a serious challenge to the Black Church. The membership of the seven historic black denominations is composed largely of middle-income working-class and middle-class members, with a scattering of support from poorer members, especially those in Southern rural areas who tend to be among the most loyal church members.[6] But black pastors and churches have had a difficult time in attempting to reach the hard-core urban poor, the black underclass, which is continuing to grow.[7] The largest sector of the unchurched are poor, urban black males, followed by poor urban black females. In past genera-

---

[4]For the thesis of the social isolation of the black poor, see William Julius Wilson, *The Truly Disadvantaged: The Inner City, The Underclass, and Public Policy*, (Chicago: University of Chicago Press, 1987). I acknowledge the influence of Professor Andrew Billingsley for his use of the terms "coping" and "crisis" sectors in describing the class gap in black communities.

[5]Smothers, "Atlanta Still on a Roll, but New Doubts Arise." *New York Times,* 14 July 1988, A-21.

[6]Hart Nelsen, "Unchurched Black Americans: Patterns of Religiosity and Affiliation." *Review of Religious Research* 29/4 (June 1988): 398-412.

[7]Laura Sessions Stepp, "Black Church Losing Historic Role: Drug Use, Teen Pregnancies Seen as Consequences." *Washington Post*, 20 August 1988, A-6.

tions some of the large urban black churches were among the few institutions that could reach beyond class boundaries and provide a semblance of unity in black communities.[8] As one pastor in Harlem said, however, "For the first time in black history, we are seeing an unchurched generation of black young people growing up in urban areas. In previous generations, you could always assume some knowledge of Black Church culture, like favorite hymns or prayers or some rituals. Today, there are teenagers out there (in the streets) who have no knowledge of and no respect for the Black Church and its traditions."[9]

The political and economic developments over the past four years since the publication of our study have only tended to confirm and underscore our concern about this trend. The recent sweep of Republican politicians in both houses of Congress and their "Contract With America" represent an intensified phase of America's war on the poor. Drastic cuts in the welfare budget and the shredding of every social program and safety net will contribute to a continuing growth in the numbers of poor people, both black and white. The United States has been using prisons as a means of dealing with large scale unemployment and poverty, particularly among African Americans who make up close to half of all prisoners nationwide and even more than half in most Southern states. It has been estimated that close to 46% of adult black men over the age of 18 are unemployed, a rate that is far greater than the official 12% to 16% unemployment rate used by the department of Labor. The undercount problem is due to the fact that the government data only counts those who are actively looking for work; it does not include those who have become discouraged from seeking work and have dropped out of the system. The high rates of female-headed households in black communities, which is now about 57%, is directly related to the pervasive unemployment of black men.[10] I will return to this issue of prisons and the

---

[8]See St. Clair Drake and Horace Cayton, *Black Metropolis: A Study of Negro Life in the North*, vol. 2 (New York: Harper and Row, 1962, revised and enlarged).

[9]Lincoln and Mamiya, *The Black Church in the African American Experience*, 310.

[10]See William Julius Wilson for the high correlation between black male unemployment and female headed households. Wilson, *The Truly Disadvantaged: The Inner City, the Underclass and Public Policy,* (Chicago: University of Chicago Press, 1987). Also see Andrew Billingsley for the growing rates of female-headed households in black communities. Billingsley, *Climbing Jacob's Ladder*:

poor later when I speak of the development of effective programs for churches.

Thus, the challenge for the future is whether the black clergy and their churches will attempt to transcend class boundaries and reach out to the poor, as these class lines continue to solidify with demographic changes in black communities and the effects of the political unpopularity of social programs for the poor intensify. A little more than one-third of the black community (ca. 37%) is considered poor; however, that one-third will be responsible for about sixty percent of black children during the 1990s and beyond. If the traditional black churches fail in their attempt to include the urban poor, the possibility of a Black Church of the poor may emerge, consisting largely of independent, funda-mentalist, and Pentecostal storefront churches. There also may emerge cults and sectarian forms of new religious movements among the black poor, similar to those exotic groups that emerged in the Great Depression years such as those of Father Divine, Daddy Grace, Mother Horne, Elder Solomon Lightfoot Michaux, Rabbi Cherry, and the Honorable Elijah Muhammad.

The Problem of Denominationalism among African Americans in a Changing Society

When independent black church congregations began to separate from white churches, they often adopted wholesale the institutional denom-inational forms or polity of those churches without much criticism. Black leaders such as Bishop Richard Allen of the A.M.E. Church were often more interested in immediately obtaining the legitimation that denom-inationalism offered than in experimenting with institutional forms that would be more suitable to the cultural conditions of African Americans. Hence there has always been a deep ambivalence towards denomina-tionalism within black communities. On the one hand, some black clergy leaders and laity were justifiably proud of the historical accomplishments of their denomination. For example, members of the A.M.E. Church have internalized a fierce pride in their denomination--"proud to be A.M.E"; it is often called the first national black organization. On the other hand, at the grass roots level, the masses of black church members often don't know about the differences between the polities of the Baptists, Metho-dists, or Pentecostals, and usually don't care. What is important for them in their spiritual lives is the ability of the preacher to bring home the message and produce that cathartic emotional crisis and response that have characterized black religion from its very origins. Church-hopping is a widespread and deeply ingrained practice in black communities; members are in constant search for the charismatic preacher, that next "son or daughter of thunder" who can help create that explosion of emotions that leaves them drained but refreshed to face another day and another season in American society. African Americans also church-hop to hear charismatic choirs or singers because music is the central constitutive element in black culture. So the denomination of the preacher or the church is not of great concern to the masses. The basic elements of black religion tend to cut across denominational lines.

In recent years we have seen the rise of a number of nondenominational megachurch congregations, some of which are predominantly black and black-led, while others are led by white preachers with interracial congregations. For example, the Rev. Dr. Barbara King of Atlanta is the pastor of the predominantly black 5,000 member Hillside International Truth Center. The Reverend Johnnie Coleman has claimed 8,000 members in her Christ Universal Temple in Chicago. Television evangelists, both black and white, have also made some inroads in the black populace. Although a study has not been done of black responses to television preachers such as the Reverend Fred Price of the Crenshaw Christian Center, anecdotal evidence indicates that older black folk tend to watch these programs even if they are members of a regular church.[11] Probably the most influential religious figure among both blacks and whites has been the crusading evangelist to American presidents, the Reverend Billy Graham.

The famous black sociologist and President of Morehouse College, the Rev. Dr. Benjamin Mays once said, "If any Negro isn't a Baptist, then someone has been messing with his religion." Mays was only half joking when he said that. Yet in our field studies of more than 2,000

---

[11]In doing interviews for a black oral history project in Poughkeepsie, the author and his interviewers were often greeted by older black residents who had tuned into the show of a television preacher. This experience also held true for older black church members in the rural South. See Lawrence H. Mamiya and Patricia Kaurouma, *For Their Courage and for Their Struggles: The Black Oral History Project of Poughkeepsie, New York*, (Urban Center for Africana Studies of Vassar College, 1978).

black churches nationwide, we saw a glimmer of truth in his statement. We found out the hard way that, in spite of the polity of the church, whether it was a connectional system with bishops or an independent congregational system, most black pastors and their churches tend to operate in the Baptist or congregational way. Historically, most black pastors have more authority and decision-making power than their white counterparts. So even when we received permission and support for our study from the Methodist or COGIC bishop in a district, we found out that individual pastors make the final decision about participation, regardless of the word from the top.

In our survey and discussions with denominational leaders among the "big seven," it appears that only the A.M.E. Zion Church, which has its largest number of churches in North Carolina, and the C.M.E. Church, whose strength is in Tennessee, have reached a static point in their growth and are on the verge of experiencing declining membership. It is significant that these two denominations, the Zions and the CMEs, have been in a number of conversations over the past decade about merging both organizations. Since I did the analysis of the telephone data for the CME survey of their clergy and lay leaders concerning the merger, it has been interesting to see that more than 90% of the clergy were in favor of merger, while the women lay leaders tended to be more cautious and fearful of losing their identity, partly due to the fact that the Zions have had the reputation of possessing very strong women's conferences and associations.[12]

During the twentieth century, the Church of God in Christ (COGIC), the largest black Pentecostal denomination, has been the fastest growing sector of black religion. The movement began in the late nineteenth century as a Holiness sect in Lexington, Mississippi. Then, Bishop Charles H. Mason led his followers into Pentecostalism after his fire-baptized experiences at the Azusa Street Revival in Los Angeles in 1907. From several hundred ardent followers, COGIC has rapidly grown into a denomination of more than four million members worldwide, making

---

[12]Lawrence H. Mamiya and C. Eric Lincoln, "Analysis of the Results of the Christian Methodist Episcopal Church Membership Survey." CME Church: April, 1985. Unpublished internal study funded by the Lilly Endowment, Inc.

it the second largest black denomination, next to the six-million member National Baptist Convention, U.S.A, Inc.[13]

There is an anecdote about this growth. The story is that Bishop Mason once approached the National Council of Churches about membership when he had about forty churches; the Council rejected him because they felt that COGIC was a cult. A decade later, Mason returned with some 800 churches and was welcomed with open arms by the Council. By then, Mason finally decided against membership in the Council because he felt their policies were too secular for those who were trying to live a more holy life.

As social researchers know and as Wade Roof Clark has pointed out, Pentecostalism is the fastest growing sector of Christianity worldwide, not only in the U.S. but also in Asia, Africa, and Latin America. Among African Americans, the Holiness-Pentecostal movement of the late nineteenth and early twentieth centuries became the carrier of important aspects of black folk religious culture derived from the syncretistic practices of African slaves on the plantations. This preservation of black folk practices stands in contrast to the attempts by the more middle class black denominations such as the A.M.E. Church to get rid of what Bishop Daniel Payne called ignorant, heathenish practices like "corn field ditties," "sand dances," and the unrestrained, emotional shouting and falling out during worship. Payne pushed his whole denomination to adopt the more assimilative norms of white Methodism, of "order and decorum" in worship and, by the beginning of the twentieth century, he had succeeded.[14] Besides allowing practices like the holy dance, gospel music, instrumental band music using drums, tambourines, trumpets, electric guitars, and bass, as well as the traditional shouting and falling out, Pentecostalism's wide appeal lies in the key religious experience available to every believer, glossolalia or speaking in tongues. While

---

[13]These totals should be taken with a grain of salt since the black denominations, especially the Baptists, have not done membership surveys. The COGIC total comes from denominational reports.

[14]For a more detailed account of Bishop Daniel Payne's influence in the A.M.E. Church, see Chapter Four by Lawrence H. Mamiya, "A Social History of the Bethel African Methodist Episcopal Church in Baltimore: The House of God and the Struggle For Freedom," in *American Congregations*, Volume 1: *Portraits of Twelve Religious Communities* ed. James P. Wind and James W. Lewis (Chicago and London: University of Chicago Press, 1994) 229-38.

there are other gifts of the Holy Spirit, glossolalia provides a continuing legitimation and an empirical reconfirmation of the believer's spirituality. At the heart of every religion lies religious experience, the individual's contact with the sacred. More than just a good sermon or a good biblical exposition, the power of Pentecostalism resides in this experiential dimension.

With this brief exposition of traditional Pentecostalism, let me now turn to another phenomenon of megachurch growth, the rapidly developing movement that I have called "neo-Pentecostalism" among black middle class denominations like the A.M.E. Church. Based upon my observation of trends, I feel that the various forms of Pentecostalism, whether traditional or neo-Pentecostal, will be the dominant motif of black denominations in the twenty-first century.

The Neo-Pentecostal Movement in the African Methodist Episcopal Church: Implications for Church Growth

It was just by accident that I stumbled onto the neo-Pentecostal movement in the A.M.E. Church while I was doing an in-house study of the Second Episcopal District of that denomination for Bishop John Adams. I came across the Bethel A.M.E. Church of Baltimore, Maryland, and its then pastor, the Rev. Dr. John Williams Bryant, who is now a bishop, and learned that the church had grown from 500 members in 1975 to more than 7,000 members a decade later. I also learned that this middle-class church had adopted some Pentecostal practices such as emphasis on the Holy Spirit and glossolalia for private prayer groups (or what I recently heard referred to as "charismatic lite"), instrumental bands, contemporary gospel music, the holy dance, and the traditional shouting and falling out. It was also a historically curious place because it was at this very church that Bishop Payne began banning all of these black folk cultural practices 150 years ago as a young pastor at Bethel, Baltimore. As the black folk saying reiterates, "What goes 'round, comes 'round."

The neo-Pentecostal movement differs from traditional Pentecostalism in several ways: first, its followers tend to come from a more middle class background (as opposed to the "sanctified" store-front images of poor blacks); the clergy also have more education and theological degrees; the churches and their clergy tend to be more politically and socially progressive; and all are activists in their communities. They combine the traditional spiritual depth of Pentecostalism with the activist spirit of the Civil Rights movement. As Bryant has argued, spirited, enthusiastic worship is not contrary to the genuine A.M.E. tradition. He claims that the place where worship has more vitality among A.M.E.s is in South Carolina where enthusiastic and spirited worship is normative and where "there are more A.M.E.s than anywhere in the world."[15] Bryant's intent is to reform the A.M.E. Church and not to abolish it.

Bethel-Baltimore and Bishop John Bryant are at the heart of the neo-Pentecostal movement in the A.M.E. Church. About a dozen of the largest and wealthiest A.M.E. churches are part of this movement, and most of the pastors have been proteges of Bryant. Most of these churches are of megachurch size (*i.e.* 3,000 or more). Bryant himself has sent more than 100 persons to the ministry in ten years, more than half of them women. This is another difference of the neo-Pentecostals from traditional Pentecostalism. By denominational rule, COGIC forbids women from becoming pastors of churches; they can be evangelists or missionaries. The black neo-Pentecostals ordinarily have a strong feminist streak, not only encouraging and supporting women pastors, but also providing nurture and support for lay women.[16] Bethel, under the leadership of the pastor's wife, the Reverend Cecilia Williams-Bryant, set up the first Women's Center in 1977, earlier than any other black or white church,

While the A.M.E. Church has been most directly affected by the neo-Pentecostal movement, there is some evidence that other black denominations are being affected by it, too. These include some Baptist churches in Texas and Georgia; the Four Square Gospel A.M.E. Zion Church in Fort Washington, Virginia; and the famous Trinity United Church of Christ in Chicago. All of these churches are megachurches, indicating that the marked characteristic of neo-Pentecostalism contributes to the significant growth of membership in black churches. In sum, the combination of traditional Pentecostalism and neo-Pentecostalism point to a developing trend where close to half of all black churches in the twenty-first century will involve some form of Pentecostalism. While

---

[15]Lincoln and Mamiya, *The Black Church in the African American Experience*, 387-88.

[16]Ibid., 268-69.

Pentecostalism may contribute to black church growth, other factors on the horizon may limit that growth.

The Challenges of Islam and African-based Religions

The religion of Islam in its various forms poses the strongest challenge to the growth of Protestantism in African-American communities nationwide. According to a 1991 telephone survey by researchers at the City University of New York, there are an estimated one million African American adherents to Islam.[17] The actual number is probably higher, upwards of seven million, if one includes the fluid movement in and out of Islamic groups over the past four decades. Furthermore, Islam has proven itself to be a viable religious alternative to black Christian churches, especially for many black males, who have experienced difficulty with normative social and economic adjustments. In fact, according to our present field research of African American masjids or mosques, close to two-thirds of their membership is composed of black men, a segment of the population that black churches have had great difficulty in recruiting. In comparison, black women make up two-thirds or more of the congregations of black churches. Thus, another trend for the future is the growing religious bifurcation of black communities, with Christianity preferred by black women and Islam by black men.

Besides the attractive legacy of Minister Malcolm X or El-Hajj Malik El Shabazz, probably the major reason for the growth of Islam among blacks has been the work and activity of Muslims in prisons and the streets of the ghetto, places where black churches have been conspicuously absent. This growth has also been fueled by American social policy in dealing with the poor and unemployed, which include more than half of the adult black male population. Rather than providing jobs or re-industrializing the economic base of major cities, the United States since 1980 has chosen to use prisons to warehouse the poor and unemployed. The major effect of this policy has been that Americans have incarcerated black people, especially in the Southern states, at a higher rate than the

---

[17]Barry A. Kosmin, Ariela Keysar and Nava Lerer of the Berman Institute, CUNY Graduate Center, "Secular Education and the Religious Profile of Contemporary Black Americans." Unpublished paper presented at the annual meeting of the Society for the Scientific Study of Religion, Pittsburgh PA., November, 1991.

Afrikaner government in South Africa at the peak of the Apartheid system.[18] Of course, the unintended consequence of building more prisons and more punitive sentences has been to contribute to the growth of Islam in black communities.

While there are more African-American Muslims in the Northeast, especially in the New York and New Jersey areas, than anywhere else, the Islamic alternative has also made its presence felt in Southern states such as Georgia and North Carolina. For example, the Atlanta Masjid of Al-Islam led by Imam Pleimon Al-Amin has the largest African-American Sunni Muslim congregation in the nation with an estimated 2,500 to 3,000 members. The Atlanta Masjid also runs one of the largest Islamic parochial schools, the Sister Clara Muhammad School, which includes all grades. One hundred per cent of its recent graduates have gone on to four-year colleges, including Harvard University.

Minister Louis Farrakhan's proto-Islamic movement of the Nation of Islam has been the fastest growing Muslim group, from a few hundred members in 1978 to upwards of 100,000 followers presently.[19] Farrakhan's charismatic presence and biting demagogic style have attracted large numbers of black people to his meetings around the country. Farrakhan's movement has also gained a following among popular rap groups that have made inroads among black youth.

Besides Islam, the hegemony of black churches will be challenged by the growth of African-based religions that are being carried by Haitian, Jamaican, and Latino immigrants. Over the past three decades, both legal and illegal immigration has increased from Caribbean countries and Latin America. New York City and Miami have been the principal ports of entry. Haitian Americans have made Voodoo, a syncretism of Catholicism and African traditions of Dahomey and Yoruba, a growing religious option, as Karen McCarthy Brown's study of Mama Lola in Brooklyn

---

[18]Lincoln and Mamiya, *The Black Church in the African American Experience*, 323-24. Also, according to the *Southern Coalition Report*, seven out of the top ten states having the largest prison populations in the United States were in the South, where blacks constitute fifty-four percent of the total. See the *Southern Coalition Report on Jails and Prisons* 7/2 (Spring 1980).

[19]The term "proto-Islamic" refers to black movements that use aspects of Islam to cover their largely black nationalist teachings. Noble Drew Ali's Moorish Science Temple and Elijah Muhammad's Nation of Islam are examples of proto-Islamic groups.

illustrates.[20] Dominicans, Cubans, and Puerto Ricans have long been attracted to the religion of Santeria, the Hispanic version of Voodoo, which has some five million adherents in the United States.[21] Among young Jamaican immigrants, Rastafarianism, a mixture of Old Testament teachings, Marcus Garvey's black nationalism, and African traditions, has made the deepest inroads. Most of these immigrant groups tend to settle in or next to major black communities, thereby providing some influence or interaction. As these groups expand from places such as Miami, they will spread their religious traditions throughout the South.

Thus, one can predict that another trend will include the growth of African-based religious traditions among African Americans. Correspondingly, the emphasis upon Afrocentrism in colleges and universities and in black bookstores has sparked an interest in ancient Egyptian religion and the worship practices of ancient Ethiopians. Historians are providing more and more evidence that the great pyramids and the Sphinx were built by black Africans. There is also great interest in black characters and African influences in the Bible. Coupled with the discovery of the earliest fossils of human beings in Kenya, African Americans are finding resources to challenge the negative stereotypes that have plagued their quest for identity.

Conclusion

In conclusion, recent demographic studies have shown that migration among African Americans has increasingly reversed and turned toward industrial areas of the South. Reverse migrants are not only coming from old Northeastern cities, where cold weather, urban violence, and de-industrialization have driven them to Southern states, but many blacks from areas such as south central Los Angeles are also making the trek back home as economic decay settles into California dreaming.[22] On the

---

[20]Karen McCarthy Brown, *Mama Lola: A Voodoo Priestess in Brooklyn* (Berkeley: University of California Press, 1991).

[21]The Santeria priestess and author Migene Gonzalez-Wippler has estimated that about one hundred million people (including five million in the U.S.) practice Santeria in the Americas. Editorial article by Richard Scheinin on Black Religion in the *San Jose Mercury News*, 9 February 1995.

[22]Between 1985 and 1990, Los Angeles County has lost 6.9% of its black population;

one hand, this reversal bodes well for the continued growth of black churches in the South because it is the region of the country with the strongest Christian religious culture. On the other hand, the South itself as a region is undergoing change, particularly from immigrant groups and their very different religious traditions.

Of the four factors and challenges mentioned earlier, the greatest challenge, I believe, will be how black churches respond to the growing class differentiation occurring in the black community. Whether and how black churches respond to the growing cries of pain and suffering among the black poor will determine if they will continue to grow or begin a major decline. Throughout black history in North America, the Black Church has been the proverbial rock of ages that has been buffeted by the winds of time and change; whether it will continue to be that rock will depend on how it responds to the poor in its midst.

many are moving to Southern states such as Florida, Georgia, Texas, Alabama, Louisiana, and Mississippi. See Kenneth B. Noble, "Los Angeles Losing Allure for Blacks," in the *New York Times*, 8 January 1995, 1, 16.

From Religion to Spirituality: Southern Women in and out of the Church ———

Nancy A. Hardesty

Women—North and South, black and white—have always comprised the majority in the church. As one nineteenth-century North Carolina planter wrote: "The forms of worship are left to the woman."[1]

While many of the issues facing and concerning Protestant women today are the same for all women, regardless of region, Southern women do inherit a distinctive history that has linked sexual and racial subordination. As nineteenth-century Presbyterian parson Frederick A. Ross of Huntsville, Alabama, explained, "The slave stands in relation to his master precisely as the wife stands in relation to her husband."[2] North Carolina Chief Justice Pearson outlined woman's role more fully in 1862: "The wife must be subject to the husband. . . . Every man must govern his household."[3] Such rhetoric was, of course, buttressed by biblical citation and interpretation with regard to both African American slaves and women of all races. As Eugene Genovese has put it,

---

[1]Catherine Clinton, *The Plantation Mistress: Woman's World in the Old South* (New York: Pantheon Books, 1982), 159, John Eppes to Frances Eppes, n.d., n.a., Eppes Collection, Duke University.

[2]Eugene D. Genovese, "Toward a Kinder and Gentler America: The Southern Lady in the Greening of the Politics of the Old South," in *In Joy and in Sorrow: Women, Family, and Marriage in the Victorian South, 1830–1900,* ed. Carol Bleser (New York: Oxford University Press, 1991) 127.

[3]Elizabeth Fox-Genovese, *Within the Plantation Household: Black and White Women of the Old South* (Chapel Hill: The University of North Carolina Press, 1988) 201, quoted from Samuel Bryant Turrentine, *Romance of Education: A Narrative Including Recollections and Other Facts Connected with Greensboro College* (Greensboro NC: 1946) 27.

the justification of black slavery derived from the general justification
of slavery, regardless of race, as ordained by God; and slavery and all
class stratification derived from the prior divine command that women
submit to men—racial subordination derived from class subordination,
which derived from gender subordination. The mouth of the Lord hath
spoken it.[4]

While the rhetoric of racial inferiority has been relegated for the most
part to beneath the surface of social discourse, appeals to the rhetoric of
female subordination are still made and considered legitimate by many
Protestant Christians, particularly in the South. They form the text and
subtext for many issues that women face in the church today.

Will Willimon said that for Southerners it all comes down to black
and white. It does, and I would suggest that, at least in part, that is a cop
out, a well-rehearsed dance. It avoids real intimacy, and it avoids real
issues closer to home on both sides. We dance the dance of race; we
know all the steps. And then we separate and go to our own homes,
satisfied that we have confronted the "ultimate issue" and can thus ignore
everything else.

The rhetoric of woman's role, as ordained by God, dictates that
woman should be subordinate to all men in society, be obedient to her
husband, take a subservient and silent role in the church, and keep to
hearth and home, devoting herself to her children. Southern icon Billy
Graham has never, to my knowledge, repudiated or amended his 1970
declaration in *Ladies' Home Journal*:

> The biological assignment was basic and simple: Eve was to be the
> child-bearer, and Adam was to be the bread winner . . . wife, mother,
> homemaker—this the appointed destiny of real womanhood.[5]

At all levels this "ideal" runs counter to the realities of women's lives today, even in the South. Thus, what at least some Christians still see as
the "biblical" role of women runs head on into major issues that concern
the majority of Christian women today: juggling home and career,

[4]Eugene Genovese, ibid., 127.
[5]Billy Graham, "Jesus and the Liberated Woman," *Ladies' Home Journal* (December
1970): 42.

dealing with domestic violence and the abuse of their children, finding satisfying avenues of ministry, discovering a theological voice of their own, or moving away from the Christian church into more congenial forms of spirituality.

Whether Southern Christians are in reality more racist or sexist than Yankees is a moot point. The fact is that the South is perceived by itself and by the rest of the country as the "Bible Belt." The South has been the home and the stronghold of Jerry Falwell and the Moral Majority, and is now for Pat Robertson and the Christian Coalition. The "culture wars" rhetoric, stealth politics, and vicious character assassination practiced by both groups have eroded respect for Southern Christians and for Christianity in general among many. The Scopes case may have been tried seventy years ago, but Southerners are still fighting to retain creationism and outlaw the teaching of evolution in our schools. Citizen committees are now attacking not only sex education in the schools but also the teaching of higher thinking skills because, to paraphrase the response of one parent in my school district, "If our children are taught to think for themselves, they won't obey their parents or believe what their pastors tell them." Whether reality or just perception, the South is still a racially and sexually repressive and oppressive society.

The Protestant church in America, run on the voluntary principle, has always depended on women to raise the money and do the work. For the past three decades, however, middle-class white women have been moving into the workforce in ever-increasing numbers—black women and working-class white women have, of course, always been there. Thus, women are no longer as readily available to teach vacation Bible school, visit and care for the sick, carry in food for the bereaved, teach Sunday school, bake cookies, organize yard sales, potlucks, and carnivals. They also no longer show up for daytime meetings of missionary societies, ladies' circles, and Bible studies. Churches can no longer rely on the voluntary services of women as so many have in the past. So who does South Carolina governor David Beasley think will do the work when he suggests that the churches should pick up the social welfare programs that he wants slashed from the state budget? I don't know.

On the other hand, many women have felt a call to ordained ministry and other positions of leadership within the church (whether this is evidence of God's sense of humor or malicious caprice is hard to tell). Particularly across the South, there have been pockets of truculent resistance to women's participation. While the United Methodist Church has led the way in welcoming women into its seminaries and ordaining them, certain annual conferences, such as North and South Georgia, have been reluctant to place them.

Denominations such as the Presbyterian Church in America have gained strength in the South at least in part because of their denial of women's ordination. While women have been given more support in the larger Presbyterian Church, U.S.A., women still have difficulty, because to be ordained as a Presbyterian one must first be called to ministry by a local church, and local churches in the South are reluctant to issue that call.

Episcopalians have found similar vagaries in their acceptance. Episcopal women priests, for example, have been accepted in larger cities such as Atlanta, but bishops in dioceses of South Carolina, South Georgia, and Dallas-Fort Worth, for example, have at times virtually refused to ordain women.

Leadership of the Southern Baptist Convention has condemned the ordination of women, but some local Southern Baptist churches, exercising their local autonomy and recognizing the call and commitment of women to ministry, have ordained them. Many of these women, though, have had to find work outside the local church as hospital or prison chaplains, pastoral counselors, and college or seminary professors. Women have found places of ministry in smaller Holiness and Pentecostal groups, black and white.

Even when women do manage to get ordained and find a church, they are paid less. A study in the South Carolina Conference of the United Methodist Church found that, even weighting the study for length of service, women were being paid less. Women do not advance to larger churches as men do. They seem to hit a stained glass ceiling.

Within fundamentalist churches, most still agree with John R. Rice, who railed in the 1940s against "Bobbed Hair, Bossy Wives, and Woman Preachers." Ironically, his own well-educated daughters (most of them married to ministers) carry on their own ministries through a magazine and conferences for women across the South. Conservative women often use entrepreneurial ingenuity to find niches for ministry while technically staying within the confines of the traditional rhetoric that bans them from pastoral ministry.

The rhetoric of male superiority and female subordination also has a very sinister side, clearly evident to anyone who reads a daily newspaper or watches television newscasts. Fueled by a biblical interpretation that tells men that women and children are their property, domestic violence, sexual abuse, and child abuse are epidemic. Of course, this is made more deadly in the South by the prevalence and glorification of guns. In Kennesaw, Georgia, all heads of households are legally required to own a gun. Boy friends, husbands, and ex-husbands regularly gun down women at work, in the streets, at the mall.

Southern Protestant churches are entangled in all of this. A circuit judge in South Carolina threw out a lawsuit brought by three women alleging that the United Methodist church had been negligent in handling their charges of sexual abuse against a pastor. Various pastors have been charged with and convicted of the sexual abuse of female parishioners and of children within their congregations. Charges have more recently been brought against a North Carolina church alleging child abuse and emotional abuse of parishioners. A married couple are pastors of the church in this case, and the wife has been the one to defend the church's practices.

Several yeares ago, the public was treated to front-page coverage in the *Greenville News* of a story in which a conservative Greenville congregation complained about a violation of religious rights when missionaries whom the church supports in Alaska had their children removed from the home. Members of the Inuit community among whom the missionaries live complained to authorities that the missionaries were beating their children—something no Inuit would ever think of doing. The Greenville church was raising money for the legal defense of their missionaries' "Christian" right to treat their children in what they argued was God-ordained fashion. It did not seem to occur to them that arguing for their right to beat children might not be a particularly good "witness" to either their South Carolina neighbors or to the missionaries' Alaskan neighbors.

And then, of course, the entire nation has condemned a distraught young mother, Susan Smith, who drowned her two sons, and yet here in the South her step-father, who admits he sexually abused her, is still a prominent Republican and a leader in the South Carolina Christian Coalition.

Southern writers are noted for the grotesque, the gothic, the violent. It is part of the South's history of slavery, lynching, castration, fire hoses, and cattle prods. And this history of violence is flaunted on the gun racks of pick-up trucks and on flag poles across the South. Southern Protestant churches still appear to carry a much greater weight of social influence than churches in other parts of the country (as Wade Clark Roof noted, there are more churches per thousand people in the South than anywhere else). No Southern politician would dream of trying to get elected without listing a church affiliation on his or her campaign literature—yet either churches are not speaking out against this legacy of violence or they have less influence than we would like to think.

The same rhetoric of domination and the same abusive consequences have been evident in the reaction to the Re-Imagining Conference in Minneapolis. The firestorm surrounding reports of the conference resulted primarily from the Religious Right's flagrant disregard for truth and fairness in reporting only sound bites and then surrounding them with blatantly false innuendoes. Many Christians in the South were alarmed by these reports because they have not been exposed to the past thirty-years' worth of feminist and womanist scholarship in religion. Nothing was said or done at Re-Imagining that was not within the mainstream of mainline Protestant thinking on these subjects. For example, womanist theologian Delores Williams' comments about bloody views of the atonement reflect the scholarship of Joanne Carlson Brown and Rebecca Parker, who argued in *Christianity, Patriarchy, and Abuse* (published in 1989) that all of the different views of the atonement, as they have been historically conceived and argued, condone violence and human suffering.[6]

All of the material concerning Sophia as a feminine image of the Divine came straight out of the wisdom literature in the Bible. Methodist minister Susan Cole (Cady) published *Sophia: The Future of Feminist Spirituality* in 1986 and *Wisdom's Feast: Sophia in Study and Celebration* in 1989.[7] Letha Dawson Scanzoni and I pointed out the feminine images of God in the Bible, including Lady Wisdom, in our 1974 work

---

[6]Joanne Carlson Brown and Rebecca Parker, "For God So Loved the World?" in *Christianity, Patriarchy, and Abuse*, ed. Joanne Carlson Brown and Carol R. Bohn (New York: The Pilgrim Press, 1989) 1-30.

[7]Susan Cole Cady, Marian Ronan, and Hal Taussig, *Sophia: The Future of Feminist Spirituality* (San Francisco: Harper & Row, 1986), and *Wisdom's Feast: Sophia in Study and Celebration* (San Francisco: Harper & Row, 1989).

All We're Meant to Be: A Biblical Approach to Women's Liberation.[8]
Virginia Mollenkott also published *The Divine Feminine: The Biblical
Imagery of God as Female* in 1983.[9] Sophia is nothing new, novel, or
neo-pagan, as the Methodist "Good News" people or the *Presbyterian
Layman* has been so quick to charge. Yet various annual conferences and
presbyteries have passed resolutions condemning all of the women who
participated in Re-Imagining as though women have no right nor enough
sense to get together and talk about theology at all.

Many Protestant churches in the South have been reluctant to use
language that is inclusive of women as well as men or inclusive of any
non-male image of God. For example, the South Carolina *Baptist Courier*
has editorialized:

> Agreed, God is spirit and therefore has no gender. But God revealed
> himself in masculine terms and referred to Jesus Christ as his "beloved
> son." We would do well to accept the same.[10]

Not only within their churches, but invariably in the public prayers so
much more prevalent in the South than in other parts of the country, God
is almost universally addressed as "Father" and "in the name of Jesus
Christ, His Son." As theologian Mary Daly pointed out more than twenty
years ago in *Beyond God the Father*, "if God is male, then the male is
God."[11] Southern rhetoric on the fatherhood of God is not accidental nor
is it without gender and racial agenda.

The South has birthed a number of outstanding women scholars of
religion, but most of them have migrated from the region to find work
and audience. For example, early feminist theologian Nell Morton first

[8]Letha Dawson Scanzoni and Nancy A. Hardesty, *All We're Meant to Be: A Biblical
Approach to Women's Liberation* (Waco TX: Word Books, 1974) 20-21; *All We're Meant
to Be: Biblical Feminism for Today*, rev. ed., Nashville: Abingdon Press, 1986; and 3rd
ed., revised and expanded, Grand Rapids: William B. Eerdmans Publishing Company,
1992.

[9]Virginia Ramey Mollenkott, *The Divine Feminine: The Biblical Imagery of God as
Female* (New York: Crossroad, 1983). She has a chapter titled "Dame Wisdom."

[10]As quoted by Jennifer Graham in "Women Question Perception of God as
Masculine Deity," *The State*, September 28, 1992, 5A.

[11]Mary Daly, *Beyond God the Father: Toward a Philosophy of Women's Liberation*
(Boston: Beacon Press, 1973) 19.

worked for interracial harmony in her native Tennessee before becoming a professor of theology at Drew Seminary in New Jersey. North Carolinians Carter Heyward, a lesbian feminist theologian, and Katie Cannon, a womanist ethicist, have both taught at the Episcopal Divinity School in Cambridge, Massachusetts. Old Testament scholar Phyllis Trible, a graduate of Meredith College in Raleigh, now teaches at Union Seminary in New York.

Women who try to teach theology in the South are often persecuted. Molly Marshall, a tenured professor of theology at Southern Seminary in Louisville, Kentucky, was forced out by the fundamentalists who are in the process of remaking Southern Baptist seminaries in their own image. Theologian Mary McClintock Fulkerson was vilified during her tenure review at Duke Divinity School. In a small victory, however, Fulkerson was granted tenure, and a professor who violated the confidentiality of certain records and used university funds to send packets of materials to seminary supporters, seeking to impugn Fulkerson's integrity, was forced to retire.

Many women, of course, do not care about theology and doctrine, but women want a story that includes us, includes our experience and issues we care about. Of course, the bedrock of feminist theology is women's experience. As Lawrence Mamiya noted, experience is the core of religion. Yes, women are seeking to internalize their own authority. We are claiming the right to think and feel and decide for ourselves. Yes, "Sisters are doin' it for themselves." (Some of us are still of that generation who learned higher thinking skills in schools, the ones the Christian Coalition is trying to ban!) We do claim our own right to judge truth claims—and we are finding many of men's truth claims false, especially when it comes to our own deficiency, weakness, inferiority, and submission. Black folks seem to be doing the same. There's an uprising on the plantation!

Some of us, to use Miriam-Therese Winter's title, are *Defecting in Place*. Others are defecting to elsewhere. All of these issues are and have been driving many women either physically or at least emotionally out of Protestant churches across the South and across the country. A surprising number of women in the South regularly worship in women's circles devoted to Wicca, to the Goddess in general, to vague forms of "women's spirituality," Christian or pagan, or to a combination of the above, usually liberally seasoned with borrowings from Native American religions. It is definitely religion à la carte. As one woman told me, "Coming here is better than church, so much more satisfying and fulfilling." I have been personally amazed at how many clergywomen, especially United Methodists, are drawn to such groups. To use Wade Clark Roof's term, these women are "seekers," questing for a more authentic spirituality.

When I asked the leader of one South Carolina group how she became interested in women's spirituality, she spoke of growing up in the Methodist Church and yearning for more ritual and mystery. So she became an Episcopalian, working for years as a professional church organist and choir director. But eventually she became unbearably aware of how the church used and exploited women's gifts while reserving all real power to men. So she dropped out and began to explore other forms of spirituality.

Another women's circle of which I am aware is led by a Presbyterian minister in good standing who is enraged by the refusal of her denomination to take feminist critiques of theology and issues of inclusive language and imagery seriously. Many Unitarian Universalist women have participated in a feminist theological study provided by their denomination titled *Cakes for the Queen of Heaven*. Conferences expanding on themes from the study draw crowds of Unitarian Universalist and other interested women to "the Mountain," the Fellowship's conference center in North Carolina.

Many women in such circles have totally repudiated their former Protestant Christian faith. Some prefer to call themselves "witches." Others are faithful Christian church members who find that women's circles meet needs that their local churches do not. For example, women's circles, usually small groups, provide a level of intimacy and sharing that Protestant church services ordinarily do not (some conservative women do find such sharing in small-group Bible studies). Particularly attractive to many women is the participatory style of ritual in women's circles, usually centered around stages in women's life cycles. There is opportunity to tell one's story, to share cares and concerns, to worship in a setting where the stories are all women's stories.

Women always have been and still are the majority and backbone of the Christian church. But women are awakening to the realization that they are still doing all the work, raising much of the money, and not receiving an equal share of the power or the benefits. Most men still just don't get it—but many women are beginning to. And many are mad as hell and aren't going to take it any more. Working outside the home and still shouldering most of the burden for the work within the home, many women are just too tired to bother with the church any more, especially with a church that demands more work and gives so little in return.

What would it take for Protestant churches to meet the needs of women? Basic recognition and equal inclusion in language, leadership, and congregational decision-making. Honesty, integrity, sensitivity, and scrupulous non-abuse from church leadership. More intimacy and honest emotional sharing with other members. Meaningful and participatory ritual. A theology that values the experiences of women and children, that is committed to racial justice and positive social action, that integrates a positive view of sexuality, and that fosters a reverence for the earth.

When women in the South do try to speak out, name their needs, and claim their own theological voice, they are met with that most insidious of Southern institutions: gentility. Yankee women are expected to speak out and to be called "loud," "brash," and "bitchy." If a Southern woman speaks passionately about an issue, she is perceived and dismissed as "angry." Southern women are expected to be genteel, never to raise their voices, never to express anger, always and only to speak soothing and harmonious words. The woman who doesn't is punished. But Southern women—both Southern belles and the good old girls—are tired of fainting, drinking, and tranquilizing themselves. They are tired of containing their anger and ignoring their own needs. Women are tired of trying to express themselves and being ignored as though they don't exist and haven't said a word. Women are tired of speaking honestly and offering their ideas, only to have their honesty ignored and their ideas attributed to a man in the group. Women are tired of being dismissed and trivialized. Women are just plain tired.

What can men do? Will Willimon suggested repentance. That is certainly a good start. Listen. Do their share of the work. Do their share of the emotional work. Bill Leonard spoke of recovering integrity. He asked, what does it mean to be a Christian not only in society but also in the church? I would add, in the home and the family?

If Protestant churches are not going to be places where women are respected, renewed, and refreshed, then women are going to continue to leave.

Afterword

Kevin Lewis

Several observations are worth adding, briefly, here at the conclusion of the volume. I contribute them as an academic eclectic: historian, theologian, critic of culture, and as an adopted Southerner.

The conference speakers were invited to address the impact of secularization as well as of pluralism in society. Each in his or her own way makes useful observations upon the impact of the latter. But the inexorable increase of secular (taken to mean *non*religious) attitudes and behaviors in the South as elsewhere is little addressed in these pages. Why, one wonders, is there not more discussion of the challenge presented to the churches of the South by this seismic cultural change in progress, a change described only in part by Wade Clark Roof as a "widening between the churched and the unchurched?"

Explanations for this neglect are not difficult to come by. The pace of secularization has historically been slower in the South than elsewhere in the nation and abroad in developed countries. And, from the evidence of opinion polls, it can be argued that church attendance and readiness to profess traditional religious belief in America and the American South in particular have resisted the corroding acids of modernity that have eaten away the authority of traditional religion elsewhere.

But responses to poll questions regarding religious belief and behavior must be as suspect as those purporting to reveal private sexual behavior. By contrast, the observable social reality clearly speaks a warning. By whatever more effective means social scientists may devise to measure it, Roof's "widening between the churched and the unchurched" is a discernable development even in the South. Likewise, on the increase is the number of the unchurched and (does this not amount to the same thing?) of those among us who, although they make occasional or perfunctory appearances in a church, find little meaning in what goes on therein and could just as easily, in slightly altered circumstances, choose to avoid church and church culture altogether. The behavior of Americans in general and in the South in particular suggests that there is less than meets the eye in the touted results of these polls. Long have the unchurched cast a sceptical eye upon their findings. Church leaders should do likewise. Secularization is a juggernaut with momentum. Embattled churches, no matter how temporarily successful in garnering their market share of church-goers, cannot afford to underestimate its threat.

How then will the Protestant churches combat secularization if not by doing more vigorously what out of habit they have always done? And what has mainstream evangelical Protestantism in the South always done or done best? In what consists its defining program, historically speaking? But then, because experience teaches ambiguity, a further question arises. What is the weakness *in* the very strength of this program, the weakness of which churches must remain strategically aware lest their "strength" betray them?

Mainstream Southern Protestantism, its "Hellenizing" liberal spirits as well as its "Judaizing" conservatives, inherits a liability for which our contributors provide too little remedy. Roof cites Sam Hill's scholarly observations on the dramatic mutual influence of distinctive Southern culture and biblical Christianity upon each other throughout the history of the region. The Southernness of mainstream evangelical Protestantism has decisively shaped the form in which this Protestantism is to be found. In turn, evangelical Protestantism has shaped Southernness far, far more than has Roman Catholicism, Judaism, or the newcomer traditions to the region marked by Roof. But, as Hill observes, the particular kind of Protestantism promulgated in this region has been disproportionately characterized by "piety," to the relative exclusion of two other important features: "religious instruction" and "social responsibility." Hill has observed that Christianities in other times and places have embraced these three main elements in more equal proportions. Roof corroborates Hill's descriptive portrait of this relatively one-note Southern Protestantism when he points to its distinctive "evangelical piety, its emotional fervor, its highly personal moral orientation."

Such an over-stress upon emotions and the self, it can be urged, places increasingly at risk the ability of Southern Protestantism to preach effectively the liberating news of the gospel in a shrinking, information-sated world. The issue is fundamental: how to ensure that Protestantism in the South will *have* a future. In our day those who choose to hold on all the more tightly to the interpretive packaging of "old time religion" handed down from the early unlearned frontier evangelists, will, I believe, increasingly come to grief in the flood of social and cultural change. Nostalgia for the past, for the *form* of Protestantism that was "good enough" for the revered forbears, must not be allowed to impede educated growth in the faith and dialectical adaption to evolving social circumstances. The egoism of over-stressed personal piety, of course encouraged by the narcissism rampant in American cultural life, can become an Achilles' heel. Over-emphasized, self-centered pious fervor becomes a caricature of the response elicited in the gospel teaching. Captured by such piety, how will one hear the inclusive message of community concern in Lawrence Mamiya's temperate appeal on behalf of the churched and newly unchurched and disaffected black commuities, or in Nancy Hardesty's passionate warning against the continuing, increasingly divisive exclusion of women from patriarchal Protestantism?

Will Willimon is, of course, correct that Southerners as a people are unique in having had to cope with social, political, moral, and economic experiences qualitatively more tragic than have Americans of other regions: the long-denied evil of slavery and then defeat in the murderous slaughter of civil war. The gospel message of salvation in spite of sin has accordingly been embraced in the region with a gratitude and fervor difficult to match in other regions. Well I remember encountering this theme as a Northern college student reading American history. And well I remember my initial response: envy that Southerners, in their historically imposed engagement with a great evil, must be a less naive, if not actually a better people for their fuller experience of the human condition. Only later was that romantic existentialism of the college student tempered in the evolving theologian by more experience of the world and of the South and by the clarifying awareness that, with John Calvin, the mind is a "continuous idol-making factory" and all are deeply entrenched in sinfulness, whatever our historical circumstances.

In this awareness, I suggest that the besetting liability of the disproportionate emphasis on personal piety and emotionalism lies in succumbing to a tendency against which Dietrich Bonhöffer warned us more than fifty years ago. The frontier-inherited evangelical Protestantism of the region is ill-equipped to resist the seductions of what Bonhöffer called "cheap grace." But it must resist, now more than ever as advancing secularization tests the mettle of Christianity ever more rigorously. Innocently and unknowing, for the most part, the historical Protestantisms of the South have embraced the assurance of total forgiveness in divine grace without responding in intellectual humility and without offering the self in the discipleship to which biblical Christianity calls the converted sinner.

If "Amazing Grace" is not the favorite hymn of Southern Protestantism, I do not know what is. Singing "Amazing Grace" can make me cry, and I doubt whether my experience is unique. The song deserves its special place in the evangelical culture and the latter-day Christian imagination of the last two centuries. (Every church should own a video of the Bill Moyers tribute to the song produced for PBS.) John Newton, the writer, worked a slave ship, after all, and knew existentially the fear that grace taught him, as he knew the relief that grace returned him upon "conversion."

But the uses of "Amazing Grace" can raise theological suspicions. The fifth of the notorious Five Points of Calvin (that is, the "Calvin" packaged by the strategizing Synod of Dort) holds that once "saved," we are forever "saved." Thus the evangelist's insistence that a convert remember the "date and time" of his or her entry into "salvation," from that fixed point never more to worry over his or her obligation under the terms of the Great Contract. Innocent of older forms of biblical Christianity, some arguably wiser or more obedient to the whole of Scripture, unaware of the lopsidedness of the region's evangelical Protestantism, the "believing" receiver of this grace has not been sufficiently urged onward to Bonhöffer's discipleship (Aldridge's "sacrifice") *and* to personal intellectual growth in the faith.

Roof's widening gulf separating the guardians of the South's "old time religion" on one hand from the "unchurched" (including the disaffected and ambivalent church-goers who follow the present course of least resistance) on the other is like the biblical hand-writing on the wall. Here is a warning surely, but at the same time, what does it mean? How will increasing secularization be heeded by the "churched" themselves?

Many in the South remember that, when inexorable pressure was brought to bear in the fifties, the racial discrimination once believed by the white culture to be defensible was suddenly seen to be wrong, changing the attitudes of many "overnight." It is conceivable, if not probable, that such a shift could occur as the changing demographic profile of the region, together with secularization, increasingly undermines the social prestige of the churches and creates new choices of behavior. It is conceivable that the emotionalistic, piety-driven gospel of Southern Protestantism, unstrengthened by education, unenriched by social responsibility, may one day evaporate "overnight." What would prevent it, in the relative absence of these missing, stabilizing elements that have accompanied the transmission of Christianity down through the centuries?

Ongoing secularization puts at risk especially religious people and institutions resistant to change and resistant to genuine, thoughtful dialogue with the genius of the evolving component cultures of the republic. Public opinion is liable to "shift like the breeze," Marion Aldridge reminds us. Such a breeze, together with the passing of another generation, may carry away even the pretense of "old-time religion," leaving what in its stead? Its leaders, adherents, and devoted friends must show the churches how and why to grow in social conscience and in knowledge both of the rich resources of their own traditions—the richness is astonishing—*and* of the vitalities of "secular" culture viewed as worthy creations of the Creator.

And yet, from previous observers we have heard that the Protestant Christianity of the South historically has not been of a kind that raises up prophets. Walker Percy once commented that the South deals with prophets by killing them off. The true prophet stands apart from the priesthood, which busies itself calling individuals to conviction of sin and to acceptance of salvation through Christ. The true prophet is not to be found aligned with the "priests" in condemning only evil in the culture and weakness in the bare, forked animal, although the prophet may well wish to include such targets of his or her wrath. To follow *this* path alone is to fall in with the vocation of the priestly defenders of true (superior!) religion, whose calling is to manipulate the inherited rites and to speak for the particular interpretation of the gospel codified by the received institutions. The true prophet, by contrast, is to be found calling into question the adequacy of the received, codified forms of the local faith and practice. The prophet's vocation is to examine closely the inadequacies of what Roof calls the "lazy monopoly" of the unselfcriticized churches.

To perform this function where traditionally it has not been valued is of course difficult. To offer "true" prophetic criticism flies in the face of the cultural belief, crystallized in the run-up to the Civil War, that Southern Christianity is more pure, more faithful to scripture, and more pleasing to God. The cultural conviction of religious superiority is a powerful element in the true (because truly ingrained) myth of the Lost Cause, and it survives as a ghost in the heightened and, of course, beneficial Southern sense of place and of pride. It survives in the churches uncontested by true prophecy, rendering ambiguous the strength Roof and others observe in the profound sense of rootedness in the region. If the writers in this volume have here and there invoked somewhat the prophetic voice—Hardesty, from Ohio, gives us a healthy dose—the reader should take encouragement to develop it further. Theologically speaking, any shift from satisfied priesthood to disatisfied prophecy *within* Southern Protestantism will help ensure a future for the churches and, by extension, for their needed work in the region.

But lastly, one of the pressing needs of the *study*, as distinct from the practice, of religion in the South is a comprehensive account of the parallel histories of the white church and of the black church that is capable of showing the intimate linkage in cross-fertilization of these two traditions. The task will not be easy, but it will become easier in time as students of the two religious histories of the two peoples in the region work more closely together, sharing their findings.

One particular phenomenon touched upon by several of the contributors suggests the promise of the integrating, synthesizing work to be done: the steady growth of the Pentecostal churches. Roof sees this phenomenon as the expression of a growing present desire for a more "experiential" Christianity. It is also, of course, but *one* way of reacting to secularization. Regardless, it should remind us of the long and continuing dialectical influence of Europeans and African Americans upon each other since both were first thrown together. White-church culture, evolving in close proximity to evolving black-church culture (both "visible" and "invisible"), has given to and taken from its neighbor, in ways both subtle and unsubtle, ever since the first cautious missionizing of the African slave communities was begun nearly three hundred years ago, and perhaps even before. Gifts of religion, of belief and of practice, have been exchanged for generations. The full story of it awaits a forceful, narrative telling. It would seem apparent, to offer illustration, that the regional Christianity of violent personal crisis and conversion, and of special reverence for the intervening movement of the Spirit (as among the Pentecostals of both cultures) cannot be fully explained or appreciated apart from reference to imported "Africanisms" shared by both cultures alike in their intimate, though, of course, troubled relationship over time. However Protestantism continues to evolve in the region, this linked heritage will need to be more fully explored.

The results may prove dangerously, creatively prophetic. The results may lend support to the churches's ongoing resistance to secularization. The results may increase reconciliation and cooperation between the races in a future promising more, not less, disruptive, provocative change.

Contributors

Marion D. Aldridge is pastor of Greenlawn Baptist Church, Columbia, South Carolina.

Nancy A. Hardesty is associate professor of Religion at Clemson University, Clemson, South Carolina.

Bill Leonard is dean of the Divinty School of Wake Forest University, Winston-Salem, North Carolina.

Kevin Lewis is associate professor of Religious Studies at the University of South Carolina, Columbia, South Carolina.

Lawrence Mamiya, the Mattie M. and Norman H. Paschall Davis Chair of Religion, is professor of Religion and Africana Studies at Vassar College, Poughkeepsie, New York.

Wade Clark Roof is J. F. Rowny Professor of Religion and Society, University of California, Santa Barbara, California.

William H. Willimon is dean of the chapel and professor of Christian Ministry at Duke University, Durham, North Carolina.